GW00690748

Modern Poetry in Translation
New Series / No.16

Edited by Daniel Weissbort

to Nell & Willem with love Tim July 2000

Published by
King's College London
University of London
Strand, London WC2R 2LS

Arts Council funded

Modern Poetry in Translation
No. 16, New Series
© Modern Poetry in Translation 2000
ISBN 0-9533824-2-7
ISSN 0969-3572
Typeset by Wendy Pank
Printed and bound in Great Britain by Short Run Press, Exeter

Editor:
Daniel Weissbort

Manuscripts, with copies of the original texts, should be sent to the Editor
and cannot be returned unless accompanied by a self-addressed and
stamped envelope or by international reply coupons. Wherever possible,
translators should obtain copyright clearance. Submission on 3.5" disk
(preferably Macintosh formatted, in MSWord, ASCII or RTF) is welcomed.

Advisory Editors:
Michael Hamburger, Tomislav Longinović, Arvind Krishna Mehrotra,
Norma Rinsler, Douglas Robinson, Anthony Rudolf
Managing Editor: Norma Rinsler

Subscription Rates: (two issues, surface mail)
UK and EC   £20.00   post free
Overseas   £24.00 / US$36.00 post free

Sterling or US dollars *payable to King's College London*
Send to:
MPT, The School of Humanities,
King's College London,
Strand,
London WC2R 2LS

Represented in UK by Signature Book Representation
Sunhouse, 2 Little Peter Street, Manchester M15 4PS
Distributed by Littlehampton Book Services
tel 01903 828800, fax 01903 828801.

Contents

German Poetry

French Poetry

Plus:

Reviews

To the Reader

MPT receives many unsolicited manuscripts, which are often inspired by an issue that we have just published. Not surprisingly, translations from French and German feature largely in our post. In the UK at least, these are still the most commonly studied languages and our most frequent passport to European culture, and *MPT* has included translations from French or German in many of the issues in the New Series. We have not, however, previously dedicated a whole issue to France or Germany, as we have to Latin America, or Russia, or the Netherlands, or Greece, or Palestine and Israel, or most recently Italy, though about half of *MPT*8 presented French poets and No. 16 of the original series of *MPT* was a notable French issue guest-edited by Anthony Rudolf. No. 16 of our New Series is devoted to both German and French poetry, or rather, poetry written in German or French, since we include an Austrian and two Francophone poets. Richard Dove's review article on Enzensberger is by way of a tribute to the poet, whose 70th birthday was celebrated in 1999. Finally we offer four poets of the "cognate" literatures of The Netherlands and Scandinavia.

We rehearse from time to time the arguments for and against bilingual publication. In this issue we have occasionally included the original text where there seemed to be a special need to do so: in the case of Ringelnatz, for instance, to show David Cram's solution to the problem of the local reference, as well as the importance of tone and its relation to form (so-called "light" verse does not impose lighter burdens on the translator!); in the case of Stefan George, because of his use of varying rhyme schemes and of alliteration and assonance, which moulds a traditional form to a new view of the possibilities of poetry.

One of our readers has suggested to us that the youngest generation of German poets is too little known in the English-speaking world, and no doubt the same is true of the youngest French poets. We have tried to present a range of poems from Goethe to the present day, and from the French sixteenth century onwards. This selection, for obvious reasons, makes no claim to be fully representative: we are in the hands of our contributors here. But it has been very interesting to observe which poets seem still to fire the enthusiasm of translators. We have in some instances offered versions by different hands of the same poet, and hope that the reader will find it as fascinating as we have to compare the responses of different translators. Nothing, perhaps, so cogently argues for the necessity and value of translation as this liveliness and diversity of response. Poetry lives and goes on living as long as readers can be inspired to translate it into their own voice – which in the case of foreign poets, often means translating it into their own language, if only in their heads. Here are readings of that kind that have been committed to paper. We shall welcome the post that will surely bring us, in the near future, more French and German poetry – with luck, some new and as yet untranslated poets. For as long as we can, we shall continue to present our choice of the astonishingly (and reassuringly) wide range of poems from many times and places that reach us every week.

Norma Rinsler

A Note On And About Menard

Daniel Weissbort

At a recent day-long British Council seminar in London, "Writers, Readers and the State", which brought together writers from South Eastern Europe (former Yugoslavia and Albania) and several British writers, translators and literary activists, the observation was made that it now seemed virtually impossible to interest the media, the quality newspapers and journals, for instance, in precisely the kind of activity that was taking place in the Poetry Library, on the 5th floor of the Festival Hall. It was regretted, too, that while some books were no longer reviewed at all, others were reviewed over and over again. A case in point, perhaps, would be the recent novel by Kazuo Ishiguro. Shortage of space is, of course, exacerbated by the fact – a fact of life! – that visual images seem to be almost as important as the words of reviews; thus, over two-columns' width of a six-column, two-third page length review of, yes, Ishiguro's recent novel, in the *Guardian*, was taken up by a photograph of the author. Some of us at the seminar, I suspect, thought we could remember times when it seemed easier to get books of limited circulation noticed, or at least when one might buy several Sunday papers, because different books were reviewed in each. On the other hand, it was pointed out that people tend to stick to a particular paper and want to be able to read there about trends, personalities and books of the moment. The circularity of such arguments is painfully apparent.

Apart from this, though, I was impressed by the discussions and the fact that visitors and Britons alike were so well informed and free of political or other illusions. One would not, I think, have been able to count on such sophistication a decade or two ago. In that sense, perhaps, the media had not done such a bad job? However, I suggested that since so many of us in the room were writers, who contributed to publications such as, for instance, *The London Review of Books* and who understood the ways of the media, we might collectively be able to influence what we all seemed to agree was an unsatisfactory situation. Perhaps there were "more of us" than we suspected, I opined.

This pragmatic (as I thought) remark, that of an aging idealist, was politely received, with a few vague nods, but hardly applauded. I had rather surprised myself by uttering it, since I am often rather pessimistic in company. I feel certain, for instance, that Anthony Rudolf, poet, translator, biographer, editor, literary and social critic, and last but not least, director of the Menard Press, would not have come out with anything so beamish. Nevertheless, after 30 years he is still giving much of his time and energy to Menard, which he founded as a successor to *The*

Journals of Pierre Menard, edited by him and Peter Hoy in the late 1960s and early 1970s. It still surprises me, I have to confess, that Menard, with its startling track record, can publish six noteworthy books on the occasion of the Press's 30th birthday and attract, as far as I know, not a single notice. It is not coincidental, I suspect, that the press is known for its dedication to translation, especially of poetry, and that five of the six anniversary books are indeed translations . . .

Oddly, although literary translation is still regarded with suspicion or as a marginal, almost sub-literary activity, it is also more visible these days ("the flavour of the millennium", Michael Schmidt called it). The award of the Whitbread Prize to two translations (Ted Hughes's version of Ovid's *Metamorphoses* and, this year, Seamus Heaney's *Beowulf*) has much to do with it, of course, although the TV panellists, at least when *Beowulf* was selected, expressed concern at the Whitbread going to what was, after all, "only a translation". I am told by Peter Bush, who also participated in the British Council Seminar, that (after years of persuasion) translation *is* now taken into account when academic promotion is being considered. This does not mean, though, that our media will give space to cross-cultural events or to publications of international interest, involving or dependent on the difficult art of literary translation . . .

However, even though I would love to indulge myself in speculation, to draw a distinction between élitism and a proper concern for culture, even in its less popular aspects, I shall refrain and instead simply mention the six Menard books in question.

The non-translation among them is the late Gillian Rose's moving sketch towards a book, *Paradiso*, written by her shortly before her death. This is the sort of text that Menard has always been open to, an awkward length, a prime and absorbing example of writing in the process of being made. Another typical (if one can call it that) Menard book is Octavio Paz's intellectual autobiography, *Itinerary*, here expertly translated with notes and an afterword by Professor Jason Wilson, and with a Foreword by Paz's friend, fellow poet and sometime translator, Charles Tomlinson. It beats me that the English appearance of so important a text should have been surrounded by utter silence. The collection is in three parts: 'How and why I wrote *The Labyrinth of Solitude*'; the title essay 'Itinerary', and an Appendix, 'Imaginary Gardens: A Memoir'. It is essential reading for all followers of Paz's brilliant international career as an *homme-de-lettres* of the highest distinction, and most certainly as the presiding genius of twentieth-century Mexican literature.

Found in Translation: One Hundred Years of Modern Hebrew Poetry, translated by the late Robert Friend, edited and introduced by his friend the poet and translator Gabriel Levin, was selected as a Poetry Book Society Recommended Translation. Robert Friend, one of the principal and earliest advocates of Modern Hebrew poetry, has been celebrated before in our journal, most recently in *Palestinian and Israeli Poets*, MPT 14 (in this anthology/issue Friend's co-translations from Arabic are also represented). As Gabriel Levin notes, the Menard selection of Friend's best work amounts in fact to a representative, though not of course comprehensive, anthology of the best of Hebrew poetry written in the last hundred years. Friend, like all good translators who have focused on a particular literature, was a natural anthologist. He has helped to create the image of Hebrew poetry that those who are interested in such matters have received. This is not a scholar's but a practitioner's anthology, even if assembled for him by another. Much water has flowed under the bridge since Friend began and it is fascinating to compare his versions of, say, Amichai, thirteen of whose poems are included, with those by other translators of this much translated major poet.

Parenthetically, I should like to draw attention to another of Mr Rudolf's virtues: he publishes not just writings but writers. One remembers his loyalty to the work of the late great translator, Jonathan Griffin, whose own poems Menard published. The press have also published Robert Friend's accomplished, lucid, sparely sensuous poetry, as well as collections of his translations, such as those of Leah Goldberg and Ra'hel.

Duino Elegies of Rainer Maria Rilke, translated and introduced by Patrick Bridgwater (bilingual) presents Rilke's masterwork in a fully annotated new translation. Again, one notes Rudolf's attention to writers/translators as well as to writings/translations. The poet and Germanist Patrick Bridgwater was the subject of *The Journals of Pierre Menard* No. 3, July 1969. This entire issue of a publication which appeared not long after the first issue of *Modern Poetry in Translation* (Menard and *MPT* belong, I suppose, to the second generation of post-World War Two literary explorers or discoverers, the first generation including such notables as the late Miron Grindea of *Adam International* and internationally inclined writers like Stephen Spender) was dedicated to Patrick Bridgwater's translations of First World War German poets (his *German Poets of the First World War* was published as a book in 1985). The Menard issue was the first such anthology to be published in England, fifty years after the end of the Great War.

For me the two most interesting books in a wonderful bunch, are: William Stone's translation (presented bilingually) of Gérard de Nerval's *Les Chimères*, with accompanying texts by Anne Beresford, Michael Hamburger, Norma Rinsler and William Stone; and *With All Five Senses*, poems by Hans W Cohn, translated from the German by his brother Frederick G Cohn, with an Introduction by Michael Hamburger.

Les Chimères is another classic Menard book, in that it not only offers these translations but invites two informed readers to respond, as well as allowing the translator to talk at some length about his translation. We are, thus, admitted into a dialogue or conversation. This sense of a creative community (usually associated with periodicals) is, I think, intrinsic to Menard, as it is to no other publisher I know. I am not, like Norma Rinsler, a Nerval expert, but Will Stone (whose translations of the German of Georg Trakl can be found in the present issue of *MPT*) has produced versions that are more than usually at home in the disputed territory between languages, that no-man's land that translators at their best cultivate. Stone neither foreignizes nor domesticates but is open to and takes full advantage of the possibilities offered by English today. He does what gifted translators are best fitted to do, producing something new, not just because it originates in another culture but because the host (target) language is legitimately changed by it. I was much taken, for instance, with his argument in favour of bilingual presentation, far more persuasive now, I think, than it was thirty-five years ago, when Ted Hughes and I began *MPT*. I will quote this passage, an exemplary statement of a translator's aspirations, both humble and proud:

> "Naturally one should, if one is able to, read the French original above my translation [. . .] It [the translation] stands alone, a sandy hummock in the lee of a granite mountain, liable to be eroded away to nothing at any time, but an awareness of its own impermanence gives it a certain daring and propensity for risk which the original has forgotten. It is this that the original needs to maintain its power. [. . .] Only the translation can keep revealing a work's concealed essence in new ways, and as layers of language slowly settle over its time-worn root, the translation accepts a truly mammoth responsibility which falls harder at the feet of each successive translator."

With All Five Senses, poems by Hans W Cohn, on the other hand, is presented monolingually in translations from the German by the author's younger brother. That this is, in a way, a "special" case, a brother translating a brother, a family affair, makes me want to hear something from the translator himself. I would have been curious to see some of the source texts, although it may well be that Hans W Cohn's work is eminently "translatable", as, say, Tadeusz Rozewicz's or Reiner Kunze's is, their language so spare and precise as to hold the translator on the tightest of reins. There is, however, a most interesting and informative introduction by Michael Hamburger, an edited and revised version of his foreword to the original German edition of this book, here translated by Stephen Cang.

Hans W Cohn, born in 1916, studied medicine in Prague, from where he managed to escape to England after the Nazi occupation of

Czechoslovakia. He trained as a psychotherapist, his doctoral dissertation being on psychological aspects of the work of the German-Jewish poet Else Lasker-Schüler. The present Menard publication is a complete translation of a book, published in Germany in 1994, of poems written in the seventies, after which Cohn withdrew from poetry. Michael Hamburger quotes from a short notice of Cohn's *Poems* (1964), in the *TLS*, written by himself. Here he compared Cohn's poems to "certain short prose-parables by Kafka". He quotes one of the poems, a fitting note, I think, on which to end the present piece:

Two mirrors sit
opposite each other
and look at each other.
Then they get up
and go their own way.
And both are thinking:
how good it is
to be in touch
with someone.

The Menard Press Anniversary Catalogue can be obtained from:
8, The Oaks, Woodside Avenue, London N12 8AR

Goethe

Translated by D M Black

D M Black *contributed translations of Goethe's 'Tagebuch' and other poems, and a note on translating Goethe, to MPT 13.*

Anacreon's Grave

Here where the roses bloom, where vines intertwine with the laurel,
Here where the turtledoves call, here where the cricket shrills, To
what grave have we come, that every God has delighted
Thus to festoon with life? – Here Anacreon lies. Spring, and summer,
and fall enchanted the fortunate poet;
Now from winter the earth keeps him secure in the end.

The Erlking

Who rides so late when the night is wild?
It is the father with his child.
He holds the boy in the crook of his arm,
He clasps him safely, he keeps him warm.

My son, you hide your face in fear! –
O father, can't you see him there?
The Erlking staring with crown and train. –
My son, there's only the mist and rain.

"Lovely child, come, come with me,
Where flowers bloom on the banks of the sea.
There are beautiful things for us to do.
My mother has golden clothes for you."

O father, father, didn't you hear
The Erlking whispering in my ear? –
Lie quiet, my dear, the whole forest heaves,
It's only the wind in the wintry leaves.

"Most handsome boy, I want you to come,
My daughters will give you a beautiful room,
My daughters will dance for you every night

And rock you and sing for your delight."

O father, father, did you not see
The Erlking's daughters beyond that tree? –
My son, my son, I saw them plain:
The old grey willows were blurred with rain.

"I love your shape; I know no remorse;
And if you won't come, I'll have you by force!"
O father, father, he's grabbing me!
The Erlking has done me an injury.

The father shudders; his thoughts are wild;
He grips in his arm the panting child.
He spurs his horse and rides home with dread;
Cold in his arms, the boy was dead.

Love as Landscape Painter

Once I sat upon a rocky outcrop,
Staring at the mist with eyes unmoving;
It was like a grey primed fabric stretched out,
Covering the world both down- and side-ways.

Somehow by my side a boy was standing,
Saying: Friend, how come you let yourself thus
Watch with staring eyes this empty fabric?
Have you let all skill and joy in painting
Carelessly be lost, perhaps forever?

Looking at the child I thought in secret:
Does this kid imagine he can teach me?

If you wish to stay thus dull and idle,
Said the boy, then nothing bright will happen.
Look! I'll quickly paint a picture for you,
So you learn to paint a lovely picture.

Saying this he pointed with a finger
Pink as any rose, across the mist-screen.
With his finger he began to sketch now.

At the top he set a sun in splendour,

Suddenly so bright my eyes were dazzled;
And he made the clouds' soft fringes golden,
Let wide shafts of light pierce through the cloud-wrack;
Painted next the delicate new tree-tops,
Fresh with their new leaves, and then drew freely
Hill that followed hill into the distance.
Down below he put no lack of water,
Drew the river in such living likeness
That it seemed to glitter in the sun's rays,
That it seemed to roar in its deep gorges.

Ah, there stood sweet flowers along the river
And in every meadow lovely colours:
Gold, enamelled glaze, and green, and purple –
All like emerald, or like carbuncle!
Bright and pure he varnished in the heavens
And the distant mountains, blue with farness –
Till I, utterly enchanted, new-born,
Gazed now at the painter, now the painting.

Have I then persuaded you, he asked me,
That I understand this craft a little?
Yet the hardest part of all awaits us.

Thereupon with care, and using just one
Finger-tip, he sketched, right down beside the
Little wood, just at the border, where the
Strong sunlight reflected from the bright earth –
Delicately sketched a perfect woman,
Altogether lovely, dressed most gracefully,
Cheeks fresh under wind-blown, tumbling brown hair –
And I saw her cheeks were the same colour
As the finger that so deftly sketched her.

Child, astonished, I exclaimed, what master
Taught you with such utter ease this mastery –
So that all you try at once you get right,
Clever both at starting and completing?

Look! for as I spoke a gentle breeze has
Stirred the air and bent the sun-lit tree-tops,
Wrinkled every surface on the water,
Filled the veil of that most perfect woman –
And, to make me even more astounded,

She begins to move her feet and starts to
Cross the gap that keeps her separate from
Where I sit beside my shameless teacher.

Everything, now, everything was moving,
Tree-tops, branches, river, flowers, and the
Veil and delicate feet of that dear woman.
Do you think that I remained unmoving,
There upon my rock, restrained and rocklike?

Prometheus

Hide your heavens, Zeus,
in cloudy vapours
and practise your stroke, like a boy
beheading thistles,
on oaktrees and mountain summits;
still you must leave me
my steady earth,
and my hut, not built by you,
and my hearth,
whose warm glow
you envy me.

I know nothing more pitiful
under the sun than you Gods!
You feed your splendour
pathetically
on expensive sacrifices
and the breath of prayers
and would starve, were not
children and beggars
fools full of hope.

When I was a child,
not knowing out from in,
I turned my bewildered gaze
to the sun, as if
there might be above it
an ear to hear my sorrow,
a heart like mine
to have mercy on the afflicted.

Who helped me
against the overweening Titans?
Who rescued me from death,
from slavery?
Was it not you, my holy
glowing heart,
who did it all?
and young and good, deceived,
glowed thanks for rescue
to the slumberer in the heavens?

I, worship you? What for?
Did you ever relieve
the ache of the heavy-laden?
Did you ever wipe away
the tears of the terror-stricken?
Was I not hammered into the shape of Man
by almighty Time
and eternal Destiny,
my masters, and yours?

No doubt you supposed
I should hate life,
flee to the desert,
because not every
blossom of dream became fruit?

Here I sit, make men
on my own pattern,
a breed to resemble me,
to suffer pain, to weep,
to feel pleasure and joy,
and, like me,
to pay you no attention!

Novalis

Translated by Stuart Flynn

Novalis, *whose real name was Friedrich von Hardenberg, was born in 1772. A friend of Schiller and of Schlegel, he studied in Jena and Wittenberg, and was acquainted with Fichte and Hölderlin. In 1794 he met and fell in love with Sophie von Kühn, who was then twelve years old, and became unofficially engaged to her in the following year; her illness and early death in 1797 determined the mood and the themes of his subsequent poems. Later contacts with Schiller, Goethe, Jean Paul and Herder confirmed his Romanticism, which was expressed in philosophical essays as well as in his best-known Novelle,* Heinrich von Ofterdingen, *and in the* Hymnen an die Nacht. *He died in 1801.*

    Stuart Flynn *has published poems and translations in* Acumen, Outposts, Agenda, Envoi *and other magazines. He lives in London.*

from **Hymnen an die Nacht**

IV

I crave the other side,
Where every torment
Will become a stab
Of ecstasy.
Before long
I will be free,
And lie drunk
In the lap of love.
Eternal life
Surges powerfully through me,
I look down
Upon you from above.
At that barrow, you shed your splendour –
A shade carries
The chill wreath.
O! Succour me, beloved,
Seize me,
So that I may sleep
In adoration.
I feel the rejuvenating
Rush of Death
Transform my blood
To balm and ether.

By day I live
Filled with faith and courage,
By night I am consumed
With divine passion.

V

You are the youth who for so long
Has stood in contemplation of our tombs:
A consoling symbol in the darkness –
The joyful new beginning of mankind.
What sunk us deep into despair
Now raises us up with sweet longing.
In death is known eternal life,
And you are the death who finally makes us complete.

Heinrich Heine

Translated by Douglas Airmet

Douglas Airmet *has published translations from Heine in* The Formalist *and in* Light Quarterly. *His own poems are included in* Idaho's Poetry: a Centennial Anthology *(University of Idaho Press),* The Temple *and* RE:AL, The Journal of Liberal Arts. *He has a doctorate in English literature, and is the editor, publisher and book-maker of The Acid Press, based at his home in Idaho, which brings out small chap-books of poetry.*

from **Zeitgedichte**

Doctrine

Bang the drum and never fear!
Kiss the maids in the market stall!
That's my philosophy, that's all
the books of wisdom sell so dear.

Drum the people out of sleep!
Drum reveille with all your might,
and then march drumming toward the light –
that's my wisdom. It will keep.

That's all wise Hegel said in sum,
the gist of books, the very heart!
I caught on quick because I'm smart,
and because I like to drum.

Adam the First

You sent the heavenly cops with a sword,
flaming and driving me batty,
and chased me out of Paradise.
That was unjust, Lord Daddy.

I had to pack up the wife, get out
of the neighbourhood, just leave;
but now that I've eaten the fruit with the facts,
I know what's up your sleeve.

You can't trick me, I've got your number.
You're small, you're just a Nothing,
no matter how you puff yourself up
with thunder and death and lightning.

O God! How pitiful is this,
your little plan to evict us.
I call it rather magnificent,
the Light of the World, an *Invictus*!

I'm never going to miss that place,
your Eden's just a crock.
What kind of Paradise is that
where trees are under lock?

I want my freedom full, without
the tiniest restraint;
or Paradise for me's a hell –
the slammer where I ain't.

from **Romanzero – Lamentationen**

Imperfection

Nothing is perfect in this world of ours.
The rose comes well-provided with sharp thorns;
in fact, to my best knowledge, even the angels
in heaven have been faulted for their forms.

The tulip has no scent. Along the Rhine
it's said that Mr Honest filched a pig.
Lucretia, had she not stabbed herself,
perhaps had borne a bastard – for a fig.

The proudest peacock has unlovely feet,
and there are times a bright amusing wife
can bore one more than Voltaire's *Henriade*,
or Klopstock with his epic on Christ's life.

The best and brightest cow cannot speak Spanish,
nor Massmann Latin, but we'll let that pass;
Canova's bust of Venus is too smooth,
and Massmann's nose is flatter than his ass.

The sweetest songs are marred with sour rhymes,
as bee stings wait to prick in honied mead.
The son of Thetis possessed an Achilles heel,
and Alexander Dumas is a half-breed.

The star that shines in heaven the very brightest
can fall, if its poor nose begins to run.
Good cider still retains the barrel's flavour,
and black spots have been noted on the sun.

And you, my honoured, noble woman are
not free of faults, not one harmonious whole.
You look at me – you ask me what you lack?
Fine breasts, my dear, and in your breast, a soul.

from **Die Nordsee**

Question

Beside the sea, beside the empty midnight sea,
stands the boy-man,
heart full of longing, head full of fears,
and dry-lipped he questions the waves:

"O answer for me the Riddle of Life,
that thorny, ancient riddle
so many heads have tried to crack,
heads in hieroglyphic hats,
heads in turbans and black berets,
powdered wigs and a thousand other
helpless sweating human noggins –
tell me, what is the Meaning of Man?
Whence does he come? Where does he go?
Who lives up there on those golden stars?"

The waves murmur their ageless murmur,
it blows, clouds over, clears again,
the stars twinkle, indifferent and cold,
and a fool waits for an answer.

from **The Book of Lazarus**

Epilogue

Our grave is warmed by praise and fame.
Stupidity! A foolish claim!
A cow maid smelling of shit and piss
who head over heels in love plants a kiss
with her thick lips againstyour own
gives more warmth than being known.
And a warmer warmth will crawl
through your intestines, large and small,
drinking grog and cheap mulled wine
as long and hard as you've a mind,
sprawled in a filthy dive with scum
and scoundrels who should all be hung
but who live, and living, breathe –
these with your sweet envy wreathe
more than Achilles whom Homer sung,
great Thetis' child, he who died young.
In Hades, questioned, he answered right:
Better a life in the upper light
as a wretched slave or a filthy dog
than here below by the Stygian bog
to rule as king of all the shadows,
your name on the lips of a thousand Homers.

Heinrich Heine

Translated by WD Jackson

WD Jackson *writes:* For the last eight years of his life – in political exile in Paris – Heine was painfully and increasingly paralysed by a disease of the spinal cord. The pain was relieved by dripping morphine into wounds kept open for this purpose on his back, but he suffered badly from cramps, bed-sores and sleeplessness as well as from the ravages of his illness, describing himself as "a dead man who thirsts after the most vital pleasures of life!" He was looked after by his devoted though semi-literate French wife, but in spite of his fame they were as short of money as they had ever been – the poem translated below as "I have smelt my way though every smell / In this earthly kitchen" being an elaborate leg-pull. And yet, by common consent, Heine wrote some of his finest poetry during this period, including two sequences in which he slips in and out of the role of Lazarus. The poems which follow are from an imitation of these Lazarus sequences (other sections appeared in *MPT* 5). However, with the exception of some slight rearrangement and one piece of commentary, they are virtually all straight translations. The poems translated are: "Wie langsam kriechet sie dahin", Weltlauf, Vermächtnis, Rückschau, Enfant perdu, Auferstehung, "Laß die heiligen Parabolen", "Ein Wetterstrahl beleuchtend plötzlich", "Die Gestalt der wahren Sphinx", "Nacht lag auf meinen Augen", "Das Fräulein stand am Meere" (the last two are earlier poems on related themes).

WD Jackson also contributed translations of Heine to *MPT* 8.

from Lazarus

"There was a certain rich man, which was clothed in purple and fine linen, and fared sumptuously every day:
"And there was a certain beggar named Lazarus, which was laid at his gate, full of sores,
"And desiring to be fed of the crumbs which fell from the rich man's table: moreover, the dogs came and licked his sores."

– St Luke 16.19-21

A sick man's time creeps slowly on,
Like some enormous loathsome snail;
But now my power of creeping's gone,
Even if I tried, I'd fail.

I know that nothing now can save
My skin and bones from the empty gloom
Of the doorless walls of the grave;
I'll only move from this room to that room:

"The way of the world is such that those
Who've got shall get (and why should they give?),
While those who have little shall lose it, and lose –
When nothing's left – the right to live."

Or perhaps I'm already dead.
Are the gaudy horrors whose shapes have flaunted
Their limbs in nightmares through my head
Nothing but ghosts? Is my skull haunted

By entirely immaterial forms?
This ancient heathen god-like rabble
Would tickle a poet's coffin-worms
With playful whispers, gruesome babble.

Or could it be I'm buried alive?
The morning comes to tell me no.
My corpse-like hand begins to inscribe
Memories of lives and lives ago.

*

Now that I can scarcely breathe
Like a Christian I bequeath –
As befits this hour of truth –
Jaundiced eye and aching tooth

To my worthy enemies: I,
Weak of limb but sound of mind,
Hereby leave my griping wind
And my grinding poverty

To the rich and greedy. May
All whose virtues barred my way
Rot with clap. Acute attacks
Lay them helpless on their backs.

Invalided, impotent,
I devise my cramps, my slobber,

Bed-sores, haemorrhoids, and such other
Gifts the gracious Lord has lent

To the comfy and complacent.
May the Lord cut off their nascent
Hopes. And when they're dead and rotten,
May their gettings be forgotten.

*

I have smelt my way through every smell
In this earthly kitchen: I know full well
The taste and aftertaste of pleasure.
I have lived like a hero, without measure.
I have drunk my coffee and eaten my cake
And taken all there is to take
From the women I've kept. For better or worse,
There was silk on my back and gold in my purse.
Like the well-bred agent in the thriller,
I owned a house, I owned a villa:
I happily lay in the summer grass,
And the lucky sun shone out of my arse.
A wreath of laurels graced my brow
And scented dreams, I don't know how,
Seemed to come true – of roses, of May –
Till I revelled in roses day after day,
Lazy and drunk on the wines of the south –
And roasted pigeons flew into my mouth –
And angels descended like golden rain,
Producing bottles of champagne.
These dreams were nothing but soap-bubbles:
They burst and left me with my troubles.
I lie here now in a damp bed
With rheumatic joints and an aching head.
And my soul is well and truly ashamed
To hear my sinful pleasures named:
I've paid for each greedy, selfish day
And lecherous night with blank dismay,
Despair and bitter helplessness.
And bed-bugs add to my distress.
Afflicted by worry, oppressed by sorrow,
I was forced to lie, I was forced to borrow
From whom I could – young pimp, old whore.
As a matter of fact, I had to implore

Them for money. Now I'm sick to death
Of hurrying and scurrying. Out of breath,
I lay me down to rest and die.
Above the clouds in the blissful sky
All Christian brothers meet again.
And so, dear friends, goodbye till then.

*

Though I can't help laughing, cloudy skies
Oppress me – till now I remember
The wind that tore at the leaves on the trees
One far-off, homesick November.

Also the pious girl who sang
The Lullaby of Later. –
I'll only stop when my heart stops
Serving as agitator

At long-lost posts in the hopeless war
Of spiritual liberation,
Composing verses for ranting crowds
Whose apparent unification

Nurtures a self-destructive greed –
Condoned by all the churches –
Which alienates and isolates.
Civilization lurches.

And yet when I'm afraid in the night –
Or bored (though only folly
Fears nothing) – it cheers me up to write
A rhyme lampooning lolly.

And the thought of ecstasy or guilt
Consuming roasted pigeon
Inspires me once again to tilt
At Christ's divisive religion.

*

A sound of trumpets fills the air:
The Day of Judgement's dawning!
The dead are rising everywhere,
Stretching themselves and yawning.

Whatever's still got legs trots off
To where the court's in session –
Bandaged in dirty off-white stuff,
Like mummies in procession.

Jesus is judge in His Father's court.
His disciples are the jury.
None who has done the things he ought
To have done need fear their fury.

Unless, of course, it's not good works
But faith which saves the spirit –
Though surely some celestial perks
Accrue to lives of merit?

At Josaphat the bodies stop.
To help decide their cases
The court orders them all to drop
Their masks and show their faces.

Only in some such summary way
Can masses upon masses
Of souls be judged on the one day.
The Good Lord dons His glasses:

Goats to the left and sheep to the right.
They're split without much bother.
For sheep shall be blessed in the realm of light
And goats shall be damned in the other.

*

Forget the holy parabolics,
Forget the pious explanations –
Can't we find a simple answer
By ourselves to these damned questions?

Why should the just man, bleeding, wretched,
Drag his cross from bad to worse,
While some happy-go-lucky villain
Wins hands down on his high horse?

Who's to blame? Is God Almighty
Somehow non-omnipotent?

Or is *He* the mischief-maker?
What a mean, malevolent – !

And so we go on asking, until
At last a little handful
Of earth shuts up our drivelling mouths –
But is that an answer?

*

Shattered by the things I've seen,
Begging God to pity me,
Begging him to put an end
To this squalid tragedy,

All at once I saw a sphinx
With the body of a woman:
Clawless, tailless, with no word-play
Turning on the merely human . . .

For the riddle of the true
Sphinx is dark as death. Jocasta's
Son and husband had it easy.
Knowledge of this sort would blast us

And our world of splendid human
Folly into swirls of rubble.
Aren't we lucky? The sphinx-woman
Cannot fathom her own riddle.

*

What lay on my eyes was darkness,
What lay on my mouth was lead.
With stiffening heart and forehead
I lay among the dead.

How long I had lain there sleeping
I can't say now for sure.
I woke when I heard her knocking:
She was standing at death's door.

"Won't you get up now, Heinrich?
Behold, the eternal Sun;

The dead are all arisen;
Eternal joy has begun."

My love, I can't get up yet.
I seem to have lost my sight.
I must have cried my eyes out.
All I can see is the night.

"I'll kiss you better, Heinrich,
I'll kiss away your night.
I want you to see the angels
And all this heavenly light."

My love, I can't get up yet.
Perhaps you haven't heard –
I'm bleeding from where you stabbed me
In the heart with a single word.

"I'll stroke it gently, Heinrich,
I'll relieve your heart of its pain.
And then it will stop bleeding.
And never hurt again."

My love, I can't get up yet.
My head is bleeding, too.
I blew my aching brains out
When I was robbed of you.

"With my curls and ringlets, Heinrich,
I'll stop up the hole in your head.
My hair will staunch your bleeding.
I'll heal your wounds instead."

She begged with such loving kindness,
Who could have answered no?
I wanted her. My body
Tried to get up and go.

My clotted wounds reopened.
A flood of bleeding broke
From my rigid heart and forehead.
And then I woke.

*

On the sands a girl stood sighing,
Wearing an anxious frown.
It almost had her crying
To see the sun go down.

My dear, though it may bore you,
You really shouldn't mind:
The sun goes down before you,
But it comes back up behind.

Heinrich Heine

Translated by David Cram

David Cram *has been since 1988 University Lecturer in Linguistics and Fellow of Jesus College, Oxford. He co-translated and co-edited, with T J Reed, the volume on Heine in the Everyman's Poetry series (1997), which includes Reed's translation of 'Der Tod, das ist die kühle Nacht'. David Cram's rather different version follows. His translations from Morgenstern and Ringelnatz appear in this issue.*

Death is the Coldness of the Night

Death is the coldness of the night
And life the sultry heat of day.
Darkness falls, and I grow tired;
The light has drained my strength away.

In the tree above my bed
A nightingale picks up the theme
And sings of pure undying love;
I hear it even as I dream.

Confession

It was very heaven when I could tame
Those dark desires of mine,
But when I couldn't, all the same
The feeling was divine.

Himmlisch war's, wenn ich bezwang
Meine sündige Begier,
Aber wenn's mir nicht gelang
Hatt' ich doch ein gross Pläsier.

Stefan George

Translated by Deborah Mercer

Stefan George *(1868-1933) is often paired with Rilke as the most impor-*
tant and famous German poets of the twentieth century, but his work has not
retained the following that Rilke's poetry enjoys. Deliberately difficult – he
refers to his spelling of nouns without their usual capitals, and his omission of
punctuation, as "barbed wire to keep out the uninitiated" – his exalted
conception of poetry and the poet recalls that of the French Symbolists. His
poems, often intensely musical, are paradoxically characterised by end-stopped
lines that create a sense of monumental fixity.

Deborah Mercer *holds an MA in Literary Translation of the University*
of East Anglia, where she is now a graduate student. Her translations have been
published in Exchanges *and she is a contributor to* Women Poets in the Age
of Goethe, *edited by Margaret Ives* (forthcoming).

The hillside where we wander . . .

The hillside where we wander sleeps in shade,
The facing-hill still flickers in the light,
And moonlight in a green and gentle glade
Is but a cloud, a floating wisp of white.

The paths into the distance pale and fade,
A whisper tempts the wanderers to stay,
Is it an unseen rippling cascade,
Or does a bird croon its soft evening lay?

Two dark-winged moths ignore the early hour,
Flit from blade to blade in flippant flight,
The hedgerows blend each shrub, each bush, each flower,
To scented distillate of grieving night.

Come to the park . . .

Come to the park they claimed was dead – and view
The smiling strands in distant shimmered haze,
The virgin clouds clad in undreamt of blue,
Illuminating pools and dappled ways.

Harvest the deep yellow, gentle grey
Of beech and box where balmy breezes play,
Of roses still unwithered on the bough,
Take them, kiss them, weave a garland now!

Take the remnants of the living green,
Take the dying asters, gently twine
Them with the purple on the rambling vine,
Softly twine them to an autumn scene.

Komm in den totgesagten park und schau:
Der schimmer ferner lächelnder gestade
Der reinen wolken unverhofftes blau
Erhellt die weiher und die bunten pfade.

Dort nimm das tiefe gelb, das weiche grau
Von birken und von buchs   der wind ist lau
Die späten rosen welkten noch nicht ganz
Erlese küsse sie und flicht den kranz

Vergiss auch diese letzten astern nicht
Den purpur um die ranken wilder reben
Und auch was übrig blieb von grünem leben
Verwinde leicht im herbstlichen gesicht.

Christian Morgenstern

Translated by David Cram

Christian Morgenstern *(1871-1914), the son of a Munich painter, was a wholly original humorist, for whom the term* Sprachhumor *(verbal humour) might have been invented. He was a serious philosophical thinker whose humour plays on the gap between word and object. Morgenstern translated Ibsen's* Brand *and* Peer Gynt, *and his own 'serious' poems are metaphysical and largely melancholy. He died, like his mother, of consumption.*

from **Galgenlieder** *(1905)*

The Pike

A pike and all his family,
Converted by Saint Anthony,
Chose to do the good saint's wishes
And stick to vegetarian dishes.

Of these, there are a goodly number,
Sea-fern, sea-pear and sea-cucumber . . .
The trouble is, such foods all tend
To come straight out the other end.

This made the pond quite putrified,
And soon five hundred fish had died.
The saint was summoned. Quite unfazed
He thrice intoned: "May God be praised!"

Das Wasser	Water
Ohne Wort, ohne Wort,	Without a word, without a word,
Rinnt das Wasser immerfort;	The water flows along unheard;
anderfalls, andernfalls	Otherwise, otherwise,
spräch' es doch nichts andres als:	What it said would not surprise.
Bier und Brot, Lieb und Treu, –	Bake and brew, love me true,
und das wäre auch nicht neu.	That would all be nothing new.
Dieses zeigt, dieses zeigt,	All this shows, all this shows,
dass das Wasser besser schweigt.	How well silent water flows.

The Sigh

A sigh was out skating one night, all alone,
    Dreaming of love's delight.
The roofs of the houses on the wall of the town
    Were shining snowy white.

The thought of his girl was so sudden and sweet
    That he came to a halt, all aflame,
And the ice it just melted right under his feet,
    And he sank – and was not seen again.

The Trellis

Once there was a trellis screen
With spaces you could see between.

An architect appeared one night
And when he saw this pretty sight

He frisked the interstitial places
And made a mansion from the spaces.

This left the trellis, like a berk,
With nothing round his lattice-work,

A sight which mortified the town
And made the Council take it down.

Meanwhile the architect had fled
From Birk- on down to Maidenhead.

from **Palmström** *(1910)*

Paintings

Paintings hung the wrong way round,
Upside down, or back to front,
Can oddly prove the more profound
By breaching a post-modern front.

Palmström is of course *au fait*,
And hangs his pictures in this way.
Himself a painter, more and more
He makes artistic finds galore.

from **Palma Kunkel** *(1916)*

The Unicorn

Unicorns, so widespread once,
Are now just pubs and restaurants.

At 'The Unicorn' we gather
To have a pint of beer and blather.

Who knows, though! Humans too one day
May end up in the self-same way,

As pubs where meat and drink are served
(Our souls and bodies thus preserved!).

At 'The Human' they will meet,
Play cards, and have a bite to eat.

The Birth of Philosophy

The Moorland Sheep just stares at me in awe
As if she'd never seen a Man before.
Our looks lock on. We stand as if asleep;
This feels the first time that I've seen a sheep.

Rainer Maria Rilke

Translated by David Hill

David Hill *translates from German, Hungarian, Romanian and Russian.*
A collection of his own poems, Angels and Astronauts, *appeared in 1999*
(NPF Publications). He lives in Budapest.

Love Song

How can I hold my soul, so that it will
not touch your own? How can I get it clear
    of you, so it can reach to other places?
I wish that I could stow it somewhere still
    and strange, in one of my remoter spaces:
some dark reach of myself, which won't appear
      to swing in concord with your swinging paces.

But everything that touches me and you
draws us together, making one from two,
    as one bow gives two strings a single tongue.
What instrument is this on which we're laid?
And by what fiddler are we being played?
    O pretty song.

Goodbye

How have I felt the cruelty of goodbye!
A dark and ruthless thing – how I recall!
It shows you one last time the beautiful
Beloved, as it steals her from your eye.

I was too weak to stop from turning, even
As she called after me. She just stayed put;
It seemed like every woman I was leaving,
That small white shape, which soon was nothing but

A gentle wave – I could no longer say,
As it waved on, if it was meant for me.
It might have simply been an apple tree
From which a cuckoo had just flown away.

Rainer Maria Rilke

Translated by Tessa Ransford

Rainer Maria Rilke *(1875-1926) was born in Prague, and lived for many years in France. Though he wrote some poems in French, his mother tongue and the language of all his major work was German. Well acquainted also with Russian and Scandinavian cultural circles, he has been considered to be the first "European" poet, but there is no doubt of his place in the German poetic tradition.*

    Tessa Ransford *was born in India, and educated in Scotland, where she still lives. She has published ten books of poems since the mid-seventies; the most recent is* When it works it feels like Play *(Ramsay Press, Edinburgh). She founded and directed the Scottish Poetry Library (1984-99), founded and organised the School of Poets poetry workshop (1981-99), and edited* Lines Review *poetry magazine from 1988 until its final issue in 1998. She is now a roving poetry practitioner and adviser (contact her on wisdomfield@talk21.com) with a particular interest in dialogue between poetry and the other creative arts.*

    The first two poems here were included in The Patched Fool, *a Morning Star folio printed and published by Alec Finlay (limited edition, 250 copies, March 1991).*

Since delight has winged you . . .

Since delight has winged you
over countless previous precipices,
engineer bold bridge now
whose arching defies geometries.

Not merely through endurance,
freak survival of great danger,
but in pure direct performance
is the wonderment of wonder.

It is no presumption to play a part
in the complex ceaseless weaving of
life's patterning, ever more intricate –
to be carried along is not enough.

Let your practised skills outreach
until they join wide contraries,
for within the limits of human touch
the god discovers his mysteries.

Dove who stayed outside . . .

To Erika Mitterer, for the feast of praise

Dove who stayed outside
returned to circle and shelter
knows what belonging means
of alien horror companions

beyond the dovecot bounds
at one with day and night
when some vague apprehension
the very sensation of flying

The most protected one
has no experience within her
to take the heart, reclaim it
challenged it is the more free

this other, never in danger
of what it is to cherish
most intimate and tender
to exult in its prowess

Spanned above nothingness
and when we throw the disc
it lands right back in our hands
pure in its own gravity

a great immensity arches
risk it as far as we can
only on curving round
it has increased.

24.8.26

Turning Point

The way from intense inward feelings to
greatness is through sacrifice   – Kassner

Seeing had been his strong point.
Stars would fall to their knees
from the force of his glancing upward.
Or he would kneel to scrutinise something
and the waft of his zeal
tired out some god, so that it
smiled at him in its sleep.

He would observe towers
until they shuddered:
building them up again, suddenly, all at once:
but often the evening landscape
laden heavy with day
ebbed to rest under his quiet surveillance.

Animals, grazing, would walk with trust
into his spacious beholding,
and captive lions looked straight at him

as into unbelievable freedom.
Birds flew through him unswerving
knowing his sensitivity.
Flowers reflected his gaze as clearly
as with children.

And the rumour that someone could really see
disturbed the least and hardly noticeable,
and excited women.

How long had he stared?
How long, inwardly deprived
beseeching from the depth of his eyes?

Perhaps while he sat, waiting in foreign surroundings
a hotel's disinterested, alienated room
sullen around him, and in the evaded
looking-glass the room repeated
and later, from the bed of anguish
again:
aerial beings were in consultation,
inconceivably in discussion
about his impressionable heart –
his heart that could feel
even through his pain-choked body –
it was discussed and decreed
that his heart had no love

(and denied him further sacraments).

There's a limit, you know, to objectivity.
And the world that is well-perceived
wants to blossom in love.

Outward-looking work is over,
now do work of the heart
on what is imaged within you,
the scenes you have captured,
that you have overpowered, but do not recognise now.
Behold, inner Man, your feminine self
distilled from a thousand natures,
the creature you only possessed before
and never yet loved.

Joachim Ringelnatz

Translated by David Cram

Joachim Ringelnatz *was the pseudonym of Hans Bötticher (1883-1934), a painter and novelist as well as a writer of verse. He ran away to sea as a boy, worked later in many and various jobs, commanded a mine-sweeper in the First World war, and later became nationally famous as a cabaret artist. Out of favour during the Nazi period, his work is now widely popular in Germany.*

from **Die Schnupftabakdose** *(The Snuff-box; 1912)*

The Postage Stamp

A macho postage stamp once tasted
The pangs of love while being pasted.
A pretty princess licked it damp,
Arousing passion in the stamp.

It hankered to return her kiss
But since its trip precluded this
Its love, alas, was unrequited.
Ah me! How often life is blighted!

The Ants

Two ants from Central London planned
A visit to Van Diemen's Land,
But on their way down Oxford Street
They both got blisters on their feet,
And so they wisely thought they'd skip
The last leg of their walking trip.

Die Ameisen

In Hamburg lebten zwei Ameisen,
Die wollten nach Australien reisen.
Bei Altona auf der Chaussee
Da taten ihnen die Beine weh,
Und da verzichteten sie weise
Denn auf den letzten Teil der Reise.

The Safety Match

There was a match once claimed it was
An anarchist, and just because
It felt so proud it went to town
And burnt a brand-new building down.

If this should sound bizarre to you
It also, as it happens, knew
The multi-volumed OED,
And got on well with A-to-B.

The weekend following the fire
It looked this friend up to enquire
Off-handedly: "To be exact,
What *is* an anarchist, in fact?"

Logic

The night was cold, the sky had cleared.
There floated in the Baltic Sea
A hair from a Swahili's beard. –
The nearest ship's clock stood at three.

In all of this there is, I fear,
Some logical obscurity:
What could this hair be doing here,
So late at night adrift at sea?

from **Reisebriefe eines Artisten** (*Letters from an Artist's Travels; 1927*)

Briefest Love

Ignorant peasants who, when meeting
Townsfolk, don't return their greeting;
Those who will not meet your eye
When nodding thank-you or goodbye;
Tongue-tied tots; shy womankind;
Old menfolk loath to speak their mind - - -

As your train goes rushing by,
Past barn and byre and field and tree,

From your window-seat you see:

These very people standing there.
And by the gate, astride the stile
Or in the meadow, facing square,
They wave and smile and wave and smile.

They greet you with a warmth surpassing
Shame or guilt.

And the purest love is spilt
In passing.

Georg Trakl
Austria

Translated by Alexander Stillmark

Georg Trakl, *born in Salzburg in 1887, published his first poems in 1908. He qualified as a pharmacist in 1910 and served in a field hospital when he was conscripted in 1914. He committed suicide in November 1914 while under observation in the garrison hospital for his mental instability.*
Alexander Stillmark's *versions of poems by Trakl appeared in MPT 8. His translation of Trakl's* Collected Poems and Prose *is due to be published in Spring 2001. He is Emeritus Reader in German at University College London.*

Alexander Stillmark writes: Georg Trakl (1887-1914) is a modernist poet who possessed a high degree of originality. He evolved a symbolic language very much his own and one which may at first encounter make him appear obscure. Yet gradual familiarity with this highly-wrought, economic style, with its patterned imagery and recurrent usages, makes him not forbidding but increasingly accessible. Trakl developed rapidly from being an epigone still largely influenced by the opulent style of Decadence, towards an individual style bearing the indelible stamp of his poetic gift: this is clear and sparse, arresting in its patterned diction and imagery, resonant and musical. The recurrent formulaic diction, novel verbal arrangement and incantatory qualities, gave him a voice that is at times reminiscent of Hölderlin, yet owes rather more to his admired French fellow-poets Baudelaire, Rimbaud, Mallarmé. Yet Trakl remains an Austrian poet and, like his compatriot and precursor Lenau, he is preeminently the poet of autumnal moods, though lacking all traces of Romantic self-indulgence. His modernity lies in the hard, almost frigid, clarity of his diction, the severely disciplined mastery of word and image. His poetic style may, to some degree, be likened to musical composition both in its formal patterning and the emotive directness of appeal. An outstanding feature is the separation of lines, phrases and images into discrete or isolated entities. Trakl's style demonstrates how poetry empowers words, giving them new emphasis and freshness of meaning.

Most poems are written in the minor key, as it were, and the translator must attune his language and style accordingly. It is also important to note that there is a refinement to Trakl's language, a dignity or *hauteur* which emphatically removes it from the language of everyday discourse. To capture as nearly as possible this rarified diction, as well as to render individual meanings accurately (ever mindful of poetic ambiguities) has been my guiding principle. The following selection represents a cross-section of Trakl's writing, the first two poems ('Music in the Mirabell' and 'The Beautiful City') being impressionistic evocations of his native Salzburg, and the last poem ('Psalm II') written in his final year and forming part of his posthumously published work.

Music in the Mirabell

A fountain sings. Clouds, white and tender,
Are set in the clear blueness.
Engrossed silent people walk
At evening through the ancient garden.

Ancestral marble has grown grey.
A flight of birds seeks far horizons.
A faun with lifeless eyes stares
Into shadows which glide into darkness.

The leaves fall red from the old tree
And circle in through open windows.
A fiery gleam ignites indoors
And conjures up wan ghosts of fear.

A white stranger steps into the house.
A dog runs wild through ruined passages.
The maid extinguishes a lamp,
At night are heard sonata sounds.

The Beautiful City

Ancient squares in sunlit silence.
Deep engrossed in blue and gold
Dreamlike gentle nuns are hastening
Under sultry beeches' silence.

Out of brown illumined churches
Gaze pure images of death,
Lovely scutcheons of great princes.
Crowns are shimmering in the churches.

Horses rise out of the fountain.
Claws of blossom in trees threaten.
Boys confused in dreams are playing
Still at evening by the fountain.

Young girls standing in the gateways,
Shyly look upon life's gayness.
Their moist lips are ever trembling
And they wait beside the gateways.

Fluttering sounds of bells are pealing,
Marching time and cries of watches.
Strangers listen on the stairways.
High in blueness organs pealing.

Bright-toned instruments are singing.
Through the leafy frame of gardens
Purls the laughter of fine women.
Quietly young mothers singing.

Secret breath by flowering windows,
Smell of incense, tar and lilac.
Silvery tired eyelids flicker
Through the flowers by the windows.

Mankind

Mankind drawn up in front of jaws of fire,
A roll of drums, dark warriors' brows,
Strides through blood-mists, black iron clashes,
Despair, night in sorrowful brains:
Eve's shadow here, pursuit and blood-red coin.
Clouds, light breaks through, the Eucharist.
In bread and wine a gentle silence dwells
And all the twelve are gathered here.
At night in sleep they cry out under olive boughs;
Saint Thomas dips his hand into the open wound.

For an Old Family Album

Ever again you return, Melancholy,
O meekness of the solitary soul.
A golden day glows and expires.

Humbly the patient man surrenders to pain
Ringing with melodious sound and soft madness.
Look! There's the twilight.

Night returns once more and a mortal thing laments
And another suffers in sympathy.

Shuddering under autumn stars
Yearly the head is bowed deeper.

Psalm I
Dedicated to Karl Kraus

There is a light which the wind has extinguished.
There is a village pump which a drunk quits in the afternoon.
There is a vineyard, burnt and black, with holes full of spiders.
There is a room they have whitewashed with milk.
The madman has died. There is a southsea island
to receive the sun god. The drums are being beaten.
Men perform warlike dances.
Women sway their hips in creeping plants and fire-flowers,
When the ocean sings. O our paradise lost.

The nymphs have deserted the golden woods.
The stranger is buried. Quivering rain begins to fall.
The son of Pan appears in the form of a digger
Who sleeps through the midday hour on scorching asphalt.
There are little girls in a yard in dresses of heart-rending poverty!
There are rooms filled with chords and sonatas.
There are shadows that embrace before a dulled mirror.
By the hospital windows those on the way to health warm themselves.
A white steamer on the canal conveys bloody contagion.

The strange sister appears once more in someone's evil dreams.
Resting in hazel thickets she plays with his stars.
The student, perhaps a double, gazes long after her from the window.
Behind him his dead brother stands, or walks down the winding stair.

In the shade of brown chestnuts the form of the young novice pales.
The garden is in the evening. Bats flutter about in the cloisters.
The caretaker's children cease playing and look for the gold of the sky.
Final chords of a quartet. The little blind girl runs shivering down
     the avenue,
And later her shadow feels its way along cold walls, surrounded by
     fairy tales and sacred legends.

There is an empty boat that at evening drifts down the black canal.
In the gloom of the ancient asylum human ruins decay.
The dead orphans lie by the garden wall.
Out of grey rooms step angels with muck-spattered wings.
Worms drip from their yellowed eyelids.
The square before the church is dark and mute, as in the days
     of childhood.
On silver soles former lives glide past
And the shades of the damned descend to the sighing waters.
In his grave the white magician plays with his serpents.

Silently, above the Place of Skulls, God's golden eyes open.

In the Village

1

Out of brown walls a village appears, a field.
A shepherd rots upon an ancient stone.
The forest edge enfolds blue animals,
The gentle leaves that into silence fall.

The brown foreheads of the farmers. Long tolls
The evening bell; lovely is pious custom,
The Saviour's black head in a clump of thorns,
The chamber cool which death redeems.

How pale the mothers are. Blueness sinks down
On glass and chest cherished by their proud sense;
And a white head advanced in years stoops low
To grandchild which drinks milk and stars.

2

The poor man who in spirit lonely died
Climbs waxen up an ancient path.
The apple tree sinks bare and still
Into the colour of their fruit, which then turned black.

The roof of paltry straw still arches
Over the sleep of cows. The blind milkmaid
appears in yard; blue water that laments;
A horse's skull stares from a rotten gate.

The idiot with dark meaning speaks a word
Of love, which dies away in the black bush,
Where she does stand in slender shape of dream.
The evening in moist blueness still rings on.

3

Branches flay windows, stripped by the southern breeze.
In the peasant woman's womb there grows a savage pang.
Through her arms trickles black snow;
Golden-eyed owls flutter about her head.

The walls stare barren and besmirched with grey
Into cool darkness. In fevered bed freezes
The pregnant body brazenly ogled by the moon.
Before her chamber a dog has breathed his wretched last.

Three men step darkly through the gate
With scythes that have been broken in the field.
Through window rattles the red evening wind;
A black angel out of it appears.

Childhood

Full of fruit the elder bush; Childhood dwelt tranquil
In a blue cave. Above the path of traversed time,
Where brownish the wild grass now whistles,
Silent branches ponder; the rustle of foliage

Alike, when the blue water rings in the rock.
Gentle is the blackbird's lament. A shepherd
Follows the sun speechless, which rolls from the autumn hill.

A blue moment is nothing but soul.
By the forest's edge shy game appears and peaceful
The ancient bells and gloomy ponds rest in the valley.

More pious, you know the meaning of the dark years,
Coolness and autumn in lonely rooms;

And in sacred blueness shining steps ring on.

An open window quietly rattles; the sight of
The ruined graveyard by the hill moves to tears,
Recollection of legends told; yet sometimes the soul brightens
When it ponders joyful people, dark golden days in Spring.

Songs of the Rosary

To my Sister

Where you walk it turns autumn and evening,
Beneath trees, blue game that sounds.
Lonely pond at eventide.

Quiet the flight of birds sounds,
Melancholy over your eyebrows.
Your slender smile sounds.

God has distorted your eyelids.
Stars seek at night, Good Friday child,
The sweep of your brow.

Nearness of Death

O the evening which goes into the gloomy villages of childhood.
The pond beneath the willows
Is filled with the festering sighs of melancholy.

O the forest which quietly lowers its brown eyes,
When the purple of its ecstatic days
Sinks down from the bony hands of the lonely.

O nearness of death. Let us pray.
This night on mellow pillows
Yellowed with incense the lovers' slight limbs loosen.

Amen

Corruption gliding through the rotted chamber;
Shadows on yellow wallpaper; in dark mirrors is arched
The ivory sadness of our hands.

Brown pearls trickle through the unfeeling fingers.
In the silence
The poppy blue eyes of an angel are opened.

Blue also is the evening;
The hour of our dying, Azrael's shadow,
Which darkens a little brown garden.

Hohenburg

There is no one in the house, autumn in rooms;
Moon-bright sonata
And the awakening by the edge of the twilit wood.

You ever think on Man's white countenance
Removed from the turbulence of the times;
Green branches gladly bend over that which dreams,

Cross and eventide;
The one who sounds aloud is embraced with crimson arms by his star
Which rises to uninhabited windows above.

Thus shudders the stranger in darkness,
As softly he raises his eyelids over a human thing
Afar off; the silver voice of the wind in the hallway.

The West
Dedicated to Else Lasker-Schüler

1

Moon, as if a dead thing
Emerged from a blue cavern,
And manifold blossoms fall
Upon the rocky path.
All silver a sick creature
Weeps by the evening pond,
Upon a black barge
Lovers crossing died.

Or Elis' footsteps
Ring through the grove
Hyacinth-filled

Dying away again under oaks.
O the figure of the boy
Fashioned from crystal tears,
Shadows of night.
Jagged flashes of lightning illumine
The ever cool brow
When Spring storms resound
By the fresh green hill.

2

So quiet are the green woods
Of our homeland,
The crystalline wave
Dying away by the ruined wall,
And we wept in sleep;
Wandering with timid steps
Down past the thorny thicket,
Singers in summer's eve,
In the sacred peace
Of the far resplendent vinyard;
Shadows now in the cool womb
Of night, grief-stricken eagles.
As gently does a moonlit beam close
The scarlet scars of melancholy.

3

You great cities
Reared of stone
In the plains!
Speechless with dark brow
The homeless man
Follows the wind,
Bare trees by the hillside.
You far-flung fading rivers!
Fearful sunsets
In tempest clouds
Inspire mighty dread.
You dying nations!
Pallid wave
Breaking upon night's shore,
Falling stars.

Lucifer

Unto this spirit lend your flame, glowing Melancholy;
Sighing the head rears up to midnight,
By fresh green springtime hill, where ages past
A gentle lamb once bled to death, endured
The deepest pain; and yet the man of darkness follows
The shade of Evil; or he uplifts his fetid wings
To the sun's golden disc and then a tolling bell
Shatters his pain-rent breast,
Wild hope; darkness in flaming fall.

Psalm II

Silence, as if the blind were sinking down by an autumn wall,
Listening with wasted brows for the flight of ravens;
Golden stillness of autumn, Father's countenance in flickering sunlight.
At evening the old village decays in the peace of brown oaks,
The red hammering of the forge, a beating heart.
Silence; in her slow hands the maid hides her hyacinth brow
Beneath fluttering sunflowers. Fear and silence
Of eyes breaking in death fills the twilit room, the wavering steps
Of the old women, the flight of the crimson mouth that slowly goes
    out in the gloom.

Muted evening in wine. From the low roof beams
Dropped a nocturnal moth, a nymph buried in bluish sleep.
In the yard the farmhand slaughters a lamb, the sweet smell of blood
Enclouds our brows, the dark coolness of the well.
The melancholy of dying asters lingers in sadness, golden voices
    in the wind.
When night comes you look upon me with mouldering eyes,
In blue stillness your cheeks turned to dust.

So silently a fire for weeds goes out, the black hamlet in the valley
    grows still
As if the Cross were to descend Mount Calvary,
The mute earth to cast out its dead.

Georg Trakl

Austria

Translated by Will Stone

Will Stone's *version of Nerval's* Les Chimères *has recently appeared (Menard Press, 1999); his translation of 'El Desdichado', the first of the sonnets, was published in* MPT 11.

Limbo

By autumnal walls, there shadows are searching
For ringing gold upon the hill
Evening clouds that graze
In the withered plane trees calm.
Darker tears this age exhales,
Damnation, when the dreamer's heart
Overflows with crimson sunset,
The sorrow of the smoking town;
Golden coolness blows behind the walker,
The stranger, from the graveyard,
As though a tender corpse followed in the shadows.

Softly chimes the stone building;
The orphans' garden, the dark hospital,
A red ship on the canal.
Dreaming rise and fall in darkness
Decaying men
And from blackish doorways
Angels step with icy brows;
Blueness, the death lament of mothers.
Through their long hair rolls
A fiery wheel, the round day
Earth agony without end.

In cool rooms without meaning,
Belongings moulder, with bony hands
Unholy childhood
Gropes in the blue for fairytales,
The fat rat gnaws coffer and door,
A heart
Stiffens in snowy silence.

The crimson curses of hunger resound
In decaying darkness,
The black sword of lies,
As though a brazen gate slammed shut.

Melancholy

Mighty are you dark mouth
From within, figure formed
Of autumn clouds,
Golden evening stillness;
A greenish darkening mountain torrent
In shattered pine
Shadow district;
A village,
That decays devoutly in brown images.

There black horses frisk
On the misty pasture.
You soldiers!
From the hill, where the sun rolls dying,
Plunges the laughing blood –
Beneath oaks
Dumbstruck! O bitter melancholy
Of the army; a shining helmet
Sank clanking from the crimson brow.

Autumn night so cool advances,
Gleaming with stars
Over the shattered remains of men
The peaceful maiden monk.

To the boy Elis

Elis, when the blackbird calls in the black wood,
This is your downfall.
Your lips drink in the coolness of the blue rockspring.

Leave be, when quietly your brow bleeds
Bygone legends
And the dark interpretation of bird flight.

But you walk with soft steps into the night,
Which is heavy with purple grapes,
And move your arms more beautifully in the blue.

A thornbush sounds,
Where your moon eyes are.
O, how long, Elis, have you been dead.

Your body is a hyacinth,
Into which a monk dips his waxen fingers.
A black cavern is our silence,

From which at times a gentle animal steps
And slowly lowers heavy lids.
On your temples black dew drips,

The final gold of failed stars.

In the East

Dark is the wrath of the people,
Like the wild organs of winter storm,
The crimson wave of battle,
Stripped leaf stars.

With shattered brows and silver arms
The night beckons dying soldiers.
In the shade of the autumn ash
The spirits of the slain are sighing.

Thorny wilderness girdles the city.
From blood-drenched steps the moon
Chases the terrified women.
Wild wolves have broken through the gate.

De Profundis

There is a stubblefield where a black rain falls.
There is a brown tree here, which stands alone.
There is a hissing wind that wreathes the empty huts –
How sorrowful this evening.

Beyond the hamlet
The gentle orphan still gathers in the meagre grain.
Round and golden her eyes graze in the twilight
And her womb awaits the heavenly bridegroom.

Returning home
Shepherds found the sweet remains
Decayed in the thornbush.

A shadow I am far from darkened villages.
God's silence
I drank from the spring in the grove.

Onto my brow cold metal steps.
Spiders seek my heart.
There is a light that dies in my mouth.

At night I found myself upon a heath,
Thick with filth and stardust.
In the hazel copse
Crystal angels have chimed again.

Mankind

Mankind before the chosen fire chasms,
Dark brows of warriors, a roll of drums,
Footsteps in bloodfog; black irons sound;
Despair, night spent in the downcast mind:
Eve's shadow comes, red coins and the hunt.
Cloud through which light breaks out,
The last supper.
A gentle silence dwells in bread and wine.
And those twelve in number there;
Nightly beneath olive trees they cry out in sleep;
Thomas, sinking, dips his hand into the wound.

Lament

The dark eagles, sleep and death
Night long sweep around this head:
Eternity's icy wave
Would devour man's golden image.

Against terrible reefs
His purple frame is smashed.
And the dark voice laments
Over the sea.
Sister of stormy melancholy,
Look a troubled boat sinks down
Under stars,
The silent countenance of night.

Heinz Czechowski

Translated by Ian Hilton

Heinz Czechowski, *lyric poet, essayist and critic, was born in Dresden in February 1935. In the late Fifties he studied at the Johannes R Becher Institute for Literature in Leipzig, then became an editor for the Mitteldeutscher Verlag in Halle. In the early Seventies he worked in the theatre in Magdeburg. Since 1995 he has lived in Schöppingen. The author of more than a dozen books, he has been awarded several prizes, including the Heinrich Heine Prize (1977), the Heinrich Mann Prize (1984) and the Hans Erich Nossack Prize (1996). His more recent verse collections are:* Nachtspur *(1993)*, Wüste Mark Kolmen *(1997)*, Mein westfälischer Frieden *(1998) and* Das offene Geheimnis *(1999). A* Selected Poems *(Die Zeit steht still. Ausgewählte Gedichte; Düsseldorf) will be published in 2000.*

Ian Hilton, *born like Czechowski in February 1935, is a Germanist, one-time editor of* Modern Languages *and author of* Peter Weiss: A Search for Affinities *(1970)*, Peter Huchel: Plough a lonely Furrow *(1986) and* Peter Weiss. Marat/Sade *(1990). He has written widely on contemporary German literature, including several essays on Heinz Czechowski.*

Nude

I wanted to give up, but
then the post came:

the past,
the cursed smell of brown coal, the
unofficial informant "Bredel", who
was once my
friend.

And suddenly
I'm afraid.
I, a piece of history and
naked.

Easy Death

In the evening, so I read,
he had stomach pains. In bed
he lay in silence, then
died in his sleep. The Cantos
were already completed, ahead
the laying out in San Giorgio Maggiore.
The gondola
carrying him to San Michele
and covered with seasonal flowers
bore a lightened body
over the water. Together with all
his misconceptions, he was laid to rest a metre
beneath the watery surface of the lagoon. There
he can now rest, to await
the judgement which will
find him guilty
or not. We know nothing except: facts
were not his concern.

The Bitterness on my Tongue

The bitterness on my tongue
Doesn't come from the orange I've just eaten.
It is a bitterness that won't go away. I can't
explain. I believe I acquired it
as a child in the war with a handful of snow
to quench my thirst. There were no
fairy tales, but at that time there was always
a lot of whispering around me: the grown-ups
spoke from behind their hands
of the war that was then being waged,
of the Black Marias and the soldiers
returning from Stalingrad minus a leg.
I saw too the block warden's
Nazi salute and heard,
whilst having my hair cut,
of the blood of Galician Jews
splattered on the wall. The almost endless stream
of Russian women in the evening making
their way up Wild-Man Hill,
as they dragged themselves from

the Göhle factory back to their camp,
and finally the wooden carts
laden with the dead from the bombing raid
    – all this must have been in this handful
    of snow, which I stuffed
    in my mouth to quench my thirst,
    this thirst as a child,
    which never deserted me, but left
    this bitterness on my tongue.

[Wüste Mark Kolmen, 1997]

Sarah Kirsch

Translated with a commentary by WD Jackson

WD Jackson *writes:* Sarah Kirsch was born in Limlingerode, a small town in what later became the German Democratic Republic, on April 16th, 1935. After school she moved to Halle where she studied biology, having acquired a love of plants and animals from her mother. According to her translator, Margitt Lehbert, "Her given name was Ingrid Bernstein; she changed her first name in protest against Germany's history and her father's anti-Semitism..." (*Winter Music*, 1994). While studying for her degree, she became friendly with a number of authors and, in spite of knowing little about poetry, began to write it. In an interview in February 1995 with the Munich author Gunna Wendt, she remarked that if she had known more she might have felt too inhibited to try to write herself. In 1957 she married the poet Rainer Kirsch and later published two books together with him (they were divorced in 1968). From the beginning her poetry concerned itself, in its inimitable way, not only with love and nature but with "unwirklichen Gestalten", unreal creatures – the invisible, the mythological, the magical. As a member of the East German Writers' Union in the early 60s, she was expected to conform to socialist realism but declined to do so. In 1968 she moved to East Berlin, where she felt safer: "The correspondents of Western newspapers were there – one couldn't go missing all of a sudden." Her writing was more or less tolerated until in 1977 she became involved in the furore surrounding the writer and singer Wolf Biermann, who was summarily exiled by the East German authorities after a concert in Cologne in which he criticized the régime. Sarah Kirsch and many other writers signed a public letter of protest, as a result of which pressure was put on her to leave. In an unpublished section of the interview referred to above, she explained: "My son was in his second year at school, and I knew that either I was going to have to bring him up to tell lies or ... All around me I could see really young people suffering from always having to conform and lie, lie, lie ... And so I went." She was granted an exit visa and emigrated with her son to West Berlin.

Sarah Kirsch has published ten volumes of poetry, as well as prose, and has been awarded the Austrian Prize for European Literature, the West German Critics' Prize, the Friedrich Hölderlin Prize, the Petrarch Prize, the Heinrich Heine Prize and, most recently, the prestigious Georg Büchner Prize. Since the early 80s she has been living in a converted village school-house in the countryside in Schleswig-Holstein, whose foggy shore-line and sodden landscapes of willows and pastures are prominent in her poetry. She has also travelled extensively since leaving East Germany and seems capable of assimilating virtually anywhere into her writings.

Although politics has seldom been in the foreground of Sarah Kirsch's writings, one inevitably finds oneself – at any rate in Germany – reading her poetry as a reaction, however indirect, to the historical events she has lived through. In *Das simple Leben* (1994) – a prose-work in diary-form, interspersed with poems, about the hardships and joys of her life in "T" – she virtually presents the composition of her latest collection, *Erlkönigs Tochter*, in this way. Her radio is frequently on, and the book includes her reactions, however brief, to the news of the time – the Gulf War and the disintegration of the Soviet Union – as well as descriptions of journeys, usually to read her poetry, through the desolated countryside and cities of the former GDR. It also provides a moving – and amusing – account of receiving her Stasi-files, including the shock of finding out who had informed on whom ("In no other Eastern Bloc country did the secret police have as many voluntary helpers as here") and "a few funny stories I had long forgotten. One lieutenant-colonel even wrote a report on how, when we were saying goodbye to Eva Maria Hagen with Moses (her son) and some other children, I went up to him where he was standing in plain clothes and almost touched him with my finger: 'Children, look at this man here: that's what a tell-tale looks like!' Or I said to another, 'Well, aren't you badly disguised again today!'" Even so, the experience was clearly a disturbing one, and a number of poems in *Erlkönigs Tochter* are related in one way or another to her "former life".

Although Sarah Kirsch's poetry developed in Eastern Europe, it is profoundly relevant as well – as I attempt to show – to the culture not only of Germany's *Wirtschaftswunder* but to that of the Western world in general. However, in common with painters like Francis Bacon and Paul Klee (she is herself a painter of watercolours), Sarah Kirsch does not consciously concern herself over-much with where her subject-matter originates: "That's none of my business", as she says in *Das simple Leben*. Her "material" (as she calls it) has remained similar over the years, but her style has gradually perfected itself to such a point that one would now scarcely want to add or remove a syllable. Syllables are in fact what she often works on. As she disarmingly explained in her interview with Gunna Wendt: "It's like doing an extremely difficult crossword. There is actually only one solution."

Naturally, the translator can only hope to give some idea of this extraordinary versification. One particular difficulty of translating Sarah Kirsch's poetry into English is that it is marked by an extremely sparing use of punctuation. In combination with her frequently idiosyncratic syntax, this helps to create a feeling that one is moving beyond the bounds of 'normal' language and social conventions. Because

German is a highly inflected language the reader is soon able, for the most part, to find his or her way around in sentences which may at first appear as foggy as Kirsch's landscapes. In English, simply omitting the punctuation – especially in her more recent work – results too often in unintentional ambiguity, lack of clarity and rhythmic awkwardness. I have attempted to solve this problem – and to reproduce the poetry's sense and rhythmical effects as closely as possible – by the use of the slash.

'Report from Munich' is a conflated and partly fictionalized account of two readings, the first of which took place in October 1993 and the other in February 1995. 'Black Beans' is from *Zaubersprüche* (1974) and 'Winter Music' from *Schneewärme* (1989). The remainder of the translations are from *Erlkönigs Tochter* (1993), the title of which refers to the famous ballad written by Goethe in 1792:

Erlking

Who rides so late through the night so wild?
A father with his only child.
He carries the boy in the crook of his arm;
He holds him safe, he keeps him warm.

Why, son, do you hide your face in fear? –
Look, father, can't you see him there?
The Erlking with his crown and cloak? –
My son, that's only fog or smoke.

"O sweetest child, come live with me!
We'll play together happily.
Look where bright flowers on the beach invite you!
And my mother has golden clothes to delight you."

O father, can't you hear the hiss
When the Erlking whispers his promises? –
Hush, hush now, child: it's only the sighing
Of the wind where the leaves are dry and dying.

"Won't you take, my dainty boy, this chance?
My daughters lead our nightly dance:
They'll love and nurse you if you weep
And rock and dance and sing you to sleep."

O father, father, can't you see
His daughters under that gloomy tree? –
My child, my child, as clear as day
It's only the willows that look so grey.

"I love you, I can't wait to take you;
If you won't come willingly, I'll make you!"
O father, he's taking hold of me!
The Erlking's hands are hurting me. –

The exhausted father races on;
He holds in his arms his moaning son.
He reaches home in horror and dread:
The child he holds in his arms is dead.

*

Report from Munich – "The Erlking's Daughter"

"... what are we doing with our art?" – Tony Harrison

Leaving the office late / abandoning the boss
On the verge of tears / where he struggles
To summon sufficient courage
To face his family – bitterly
Blaming the bureaucratic
Liquidation / the "re-engineering" /
Of his entire department / on everyone
Apart from himself – I hurriedly
Stride into / and nearly
Knock over / a Spanish
Colleague / I've been unable
To prevent myself from finding
Attractive / so distraught that
She's misplaced her car-keys / somewhere
In our exceedingly spacious / and
Correspondingly expensive / open-plan
Office / where more than keys
Have gone astray / and which compels you
To lower your voice / whenever
You want to gossip behind the boss's
Or some unprepossessing colleague's
Back. And she
Is also on the verge of

Tears. But this institutionalized
Meat-machine won't miss
Us / and I stifle
An impulse to help her / mumbling
Excuses for having to dash / as I dash
Away down well-hoovered labyrinths
Of anonymous corridors. Outside the rain
(November it was / And the wind tore
At the leaves) cools me / as I
Glance up – as I usually do – in unwilling
Awe / at the glass-and-metal mountain of
The Hypo-Bank HQ / (how reassuring
It used to be / all
That money) / before hurrying on
Into Munich's newest and shiniest /
Still thoroughly polished / and even more
Thoroughly policed / U-Bahn. *But today*
A small disturbance. The wife
Of a Turkish Gastarbeiter *– or so she seems –*
Is shouting and spitting venomously
At anyone coming too near. Angst
Essen Seele Auf / *said Rainer Werner*
Fassbinder – that mythical
Monster / sighted on rare
Occasions / bad-temperedly munching
Apples / along the Clemens-
Straße in Schwabing / before the heel of
Bavaria crushed him. Er war eh
Ein großes Schwein / *smirked*
A colleague by the name of Würstl. Und du
Bist ein kleines Würstel / *giggled*
Our secretary. But now I am
Embarrassed / to see my Spanish
Colleague / drifting along the platform /
As if in a nightmare / even
Closer to tears / with her hair
Distinctly wet / and wearing
A blouse and slacks. Could it be
Her coat is locked in her car? The wife
Of the Turkish Gastarbeiter */ sensing*
Her weakness / spits and shouts
At her / with particularly vicious
Aggression / so that she jumps
With fright. I heartlessly avoid her

As the train pulls up / by
Getting into another
Compartment. But I hope (I tell myself)
She won't catch cold. Relieved
Not to see her / alighting
At Odeonsplatz / I've problems enough
Of my own / I catch myself
Thinking. At the top of the escalators
The rain is heavier. Beyond the Hofgarten
The Military Museum / until
Lately a bomb-damaged
Ruin / (Lest we
Should fail to remember!) / *shines forth –*
A bureaucrat's paradise. Behind me
Is where (I find it hard
To forget) a line of policemen
Broke up the November putsch / only
Three score years and ten
Ago. The first to fall was
Arm-in-arm with Hitler / whose shoulder
Was dislocated. Within a minute / nineteen
Nazis and police lay dead. The Führer
Escaped to Uffing / where he was later
Arrested. And that
Was the end of him. *Or so everyone*
Thought. But if I'm not to be late
For the poetry reading / I'll have to
Hurry again. I'm also hungry and thirsty and
Tired of my heavy
Briefcase. And everywhere's
Closed: expensive shops / exclusive
Cafés: nothing for the likes of me / still
Stinking of office / not
A kiosk or McDonald's / around
Here anywhere. I pass
The Hypo-Bank Foundation / which, like
It or not / puts on the best
Exhibitions in Munich / and hurry
Through the rain and darkness / of the empty
Pedestrian precinct / in search of
Food. In my rumbling ears
I only slowly perceive
The music – a piece for Spanish
Guitar and violin / by

Villa-Lobos, perhaps – emanating strangely
From nowhere at all / or so it seems
For a moment / until I realize
It must be buskers. And there they
Are: two students sheltering under
An arcade / between a chic
Boutique / and a glossy
Shop like a box of chocolates / displaying
Individually decorated
Pralines / Negerküsse / truffles
And other goodies / fit
For a Chancellor. They look
Too cold / and their jackets
Too thin / to be able to twangle
So warm an air. Yet only a couple
Of minutes further / and as if by magic
An invisible flautist
Plays Mozart from round the corner
Of another arcade / whose brilliant windows
Are crowded with Bavarian
Costumes / exorbitantly priced Leder-
Hosen / and Tyrolean hats with
Chamois beards. So much talent
Playing for no one! – not even me / who
Pass by on the other side / in too much of a hurry
(I tell myself) for hand-outs / and shortly arrive
Fifteen unbelievable minutes early / at
The brightly lit / multi-storey
Bookshop / where Sarah
Kirsch / who lives beside
The tar-black sea / in far-away
Schleswig-Holstein / is scheduled
To read her luminous poems. Clutching
My briefcase / despite official
Attempts / to consign it plus irreplaceable
Contents / to a heaped-up
Cloakroom / I join the audience
Of maybe two hundred / mainly middle-aged
To elderly / professional or executive
Persons / unlikely book-
Lifters anyway / I'd
've thought. Once seated / I unobtrusively
Position my folded coat / in front of
My rumbling stomach / in the hope of

Muffling it / and glance again at
Schwarze Bohnen / *which so beguiled*
Me yesterday afternoon / Sunday
Afternoon / when I first read it
At home / that here I am
Today:

Black Beans

Afternoons my hand takes up a book /
Afternoons my hand puts down a book /
Afternoons I remember there's a war on /
Afternoons I forget about War /
Afternoons I grind the coffee /
Afternoons I put the ground-down coffee
Back together / lovely
Black beans /
Afternoons I undress myself / dress myself /
First make up my face / then wash it /
Sing / am silent.

And as yesterday / the afternoon
Darkened into wintry silence:

Winter Music

Once I was a red
Vixen / by springing high
I got what I wanted.

Grey I am now: grey rain.
I have come as far as Greenland
In my heart.

On the coast a stone is shining.
On it is written: *No one returns.*
The stone foreshortens my life.

The four ends of the earth
Are filled with suffering. Love
Is like breaking your spine.

Love? And natural human faith
In inhuman institutions? And hope
For peace in this iron time / of
Technological know-how – of
Doubts, disputes, distractions,
Benumbing our souls? I wonder
Whether my broken-backed boss
Is still in his office – still
In tears. But now a not at all
Tearful Frau Kirsch / looking grim
And displeased / is ready
To read. The book-shop manager – looking
Nervous and ill-at-ease – explains
That Fr. Kirsch's publisher / for private
And personal reasons / has been unable
To show up (all the way from
Stuttgart) / and it has therefore
Devolved upon his own unworthy
(= Unwilling) head to do the honours. One has
The impression / he has neglected
To read the actual books / of
The distinguished poet (= mythical
Monster) / scowling beside him. But
He's got plenty for sale / as he
Disarmingly informs us. Also
Fr. Kirsch's watercolours are
For sale. And he invites us
(Twice) to "admire" them / after
She's read / from The Erlking's
Daughter */ which this unfriendly*
Lady / now brusquely proceeds to
Do / by throwing
Her gleaming, colourful poems
Away / like seed-corn on a stony
Field / let them root or rot. Yet gradually
She begins to glow / or to lose herself
In those mysterious, angry, amusing,
Glinting words. But without a sign
Of condescension. And as for
Performance / the audience, bewitched
And entirely silent / straining to hear
Each accent / each pause /
Might just as well

Be entirely elsewhere. Or
Dead. Or a part of
Her art:

Mudflats I

Salt-stains on my boots / I hurried
Away beneath the beacon. The tide-line
Heaps itself morosely to-
Gether: sea-grass, seagull-wings /
Plastic rubbish, age-old shell-money / in
Between a few scattered stars.
The channels glimmer like a deep
Memory. The slender sickle
Of the moon / went pissing off keenly
Through the plundered heavens: I couldn't
Free my feet / and oozed along
As though Caspar David's
Inferior cousin /
Had painted me to the shore / with pitch.
From the islands resounded
The honking of geese.

Mudflats II

When Fortune brought me together
Again with Elke / she said
The red-sky-at-night wasn't purple
Red / as she'd believed / but
Soft silky yellow / the ooze of
The mudflats looked just like
Violet-filled meadows / or the crocuses
At the castle in Husum / and the evening glow
Like Doomsday in winter at
Four / before it snows Father Xmases.

Mudflats III

I, the Erlking's daughter / have an
Important appointment / with two
Apocalyptical Riders out on the mud / a

Tête-à-tête on shaky ground /
Now before day-break reddens.
Swirls of smoky fog / surprisingly
Hasty snow / create a nice
Sense of obligation / which imposes itself
On seagull-carcasses / coke-tins. The
Faded moon on its speedy way /
Between copulating clouds / declares
An admiration for the albatross / as it
Flies up from the South / while Jupiter
Illuminates the cow-shed / and then the oil-rig.
Happy *Neujahr!* signal the distress-flares /
And the boy from Büsum will never
Be found. The crows are falling /
Black apples / from the only tree.

Reeling off her darkly
Sparkling lines / she reads of melancholy, wintry,
Wind-blown, lonely places. Of lemon-faced,
Waiting, cruel,
Disappointed people. And
Of furry, hungry, hunting,
Hunted creatures. Her world is
Hostile, secretive, beautiful
And indifferent. Our lives are isolated,
Painful, amusing, violent:

Wall

On this side it was colourful / windows and doors /
Rebellious ladders / Icarus
Wings chimerically painted at
One point / and me as well / beside
My unshocked child / as one day we
Came through it with a
Caseful of toys – Russian
Swords / Mongolian kettles / falling
Out of it – a typewriter / half-finished
Love-stories still stuck in the
Roller / and a couple of friendly
Postcards from Ellis and Franz / who came to stay
Twice more / before he ended under

The sod at Märkisch-Buchholz / I probably didn't
Look back / continued shaking
My head in an orderly manner / leapt
Straight for Marina and Edith's old
Banger / our sisters go in
Colourful clothes / showed me a
Paperwhite garden / between North and
Night / on the ground were lying
The crown-like hats.

Iceland

A white threadbare sun goes out /
On the snowdrifts caws / in deepest
Disdain / the rune of darkness /
The stormy air
Sings gruesome songs.

Our land is completely sea-
Locked / heart-ache waxes
As the light sinks. Our
Poets write elegies / o
Summer so short – so drunken – and gone.

Spring-Tide I

It smells of sea-weed / salt and truth /
The sky writes letters of farewell /
Repetitions of something which never
Came true / old fishermen / now
Emptying the mussel-beds /
Have octopus and frightened
Shark in their nets / the light
Sinks here by itself / and out
Leaps the lion / on target.

Winter-Garden I

I lie stretched out beneath the ice
In a skin of transparent light.
The fish bump into it, the sun

Stands over it. I feel the hedge-
King the wren's sharp songs. Black crashing
Windy night reigns longer.
Roaring and breaking of ice. The sea
Lies heavy on me and the land.

And as she read "Black crashing
Windy night" / black
Crashing windy night announced
Its presence / by suddenly
Howling / rattling the
Windows / lighting the city-
Skyline with crackling flashes / followed
By claps of thunder / as if
In cosmic approval / then
Great swirls of snow. For a second
The lights go out / to a tremendous
Bang they flicker back on. Without
A pause / without as much as
Looking up / she raises her right
Hand in unsurprised – not
Unamused – acknowledgement / and
Continues:

Winter-Garden II

In the meantime we've all
Started drinking in here.
The trees and stags in the
Wall-paper long to get
Out into the open.

Windows and doors are
For ever bolted and
Completely barred. No one
Can say which season
Reigns.

And how my heart races! Does it beat
For fear or longing? I only
Know I'm waiting for something / either
For you or death.

Ah, how unhappy we
All are and smoke
Strong benumbing stuff.

Later

The candles flicker in the garden
While the guests slowly
Withdraw. Disguised
As a farmer / I stalk behind the

Hedge. A preparation for
Something that never happens.

Long Winter

Came like the
Star of Bethlehem.
To keep warm we burned
Telegraph-poles. O
Horror / all the
Snarling pumpkins.

Prussian files
Called up my in-
Come for
Copies.

And yet we
Had a great
Time / as if at a
Chameleon-wedding.

The Other World

I am the ox of seven battles
In the ruinous state my homeland.
A steadfast Eber I was / am
The murmur of gentle rivers and free.

Fugitive

Running ahead
Of myself / I made off / telling
Myself: for-
Get! And be
Hard. That's how to

Report on earth. On the
Not indescribable
Trees / as summer
Begins.

What I Learned In Norway

All cats have thick
Angora fur /
Horses a
Shaggy horse-coat / even the
People
Are hugely hairy. The further
North you go the more
Exciting grows
The fur. In Tromsø
I dined with a
Bear and went
Unclothed.

Malmö Blessing

In Malmö / the nightin-
Gales sing the souls out of
Their hearts / and the Baltic poets
Are totally drunk on
Feeling free / the chance of
Travelling at last / O God

Reward them for their half-
Wasted lives / a thousand
Baltic elegies / and may this
Lovely turquoise-green sea /
Which once leapt over

My own little bootees / make them

Immune against betrayal
And velvet speech.

Letter

It's very nice now when it
Gets dark. I sleep with my
Feet towards the sea / at my back
The mountains. Straight ahead lies America.
In the market-place there are holes
Still from our bombs on Swansea.

Emmanuel College

Ravens with great gobbets in
Their beaks / fly over the green
Green grass / the pond's narcissi.
Have they done in a student /
Shared out a Master of Arts /
I wonder / as my terrible
Toast is wheeled in.

Highland

I see myself on the banks
Of Loch Lomond: the vernal
Waterfalls startle / blowing
Their trumpets from
The slopes. My melancholy
Bog-heart forgets its croaking.

Northern June

The nights have lost their
Nightness: white
Steps / the
Horizon's rust-
Red hangings.

Whoever leaps here
Could be happy henceforth.
Thrice I call you / but

You are not
On earth.

Earth-Love

Even the hunchback having a fit
Is beautiful in such a landscape /
Its green air softly sinking
To the earth / big birds standing in trees
Higher than clouds / when waggoners drive
Muck-spreaders from night till morning /
Their powerful double-fantasies
Infiltrate my dreams / faded memories
Of fifteen forgotten men / and only
The corresponding landscapes remain
In my mind / in fact no one
Can sleep around here / and no
Wonder in such amazingly lit-up
Nights / the only wonder's my
Life / and had it not been for the muck-
Spreader-drivers / who now
With stubbly beards and rolled-up
Sleeves approach each other / blocking
The only way between moors / it might have
Been possible to meet one's own little
Death now / which will sprout in this
Fertile land / where normally
Beings exist / whose cold pupils
Cause pitch-forks raised in self-defence
To sink / as further on
Sea-wind the yachts of townsfolk.

He Shall Be Called Jewel

The kingfisher left the nest
For the first time / fluttered among
Twigs / while behind the
Millstone / the cunning

Old cat lies waiting. A waste
Of beautiful colours / recently acquired
Grace.

Creatures

Night-time. In the distance across the plain
A single light. I imagine
People flicking it on /
A large and fun-loving family /
And assorted motives / including love /
Jealousy / madness / death. It could also
Be the birth of an animal / very
Likely in such an area / at
This time of year. All-considering, sifting
The possibilities / is it a calf / is it a
Pig / male or female / or a
Hybrid – the superbly equipped
Inhabitants of the house / the cow-sheds / the
Owners of the light / remain the object
Of my concern / until their lamp
Goes out. Then they are all
Dead to me.

Angel

Before I
Write my own untruths
In stone / or
Sow them in frozen
Earth:

Your house stands
On the brim of the world / I pass
Through its empty garden.
The window burns red /
I am as deathly pale
As fallen snow.

Destination

Now from the leaves of the birch-tree
A sea of foliage swathes us.
We await an epiphany.
We have gathered beneath the
Exorcising oak / stare
Into the sinking sun. Gently
Death our Lord appears.

Celtic

I see an earth I don't
Like the look of / summer
Birdless / cows
Milkless / men
Gutless / think I'd
Rather! say farewell.

Derision

The wind bashes
The door against my
Head: thus summer
Takes
Its leave.

Yellow

The foolish yellow of the water-lilies /
The dark the all-agreeing river.
Autumn sings its dirge to me
Half the night in the chimney.

She pauses at last / raising her eyes
From her MSS / and acknowledges / almost
Smilingly / our existence –
Inquiring are there
Any / we'd like to hear
Again. Gleich alle! someone says

At once. Outside the storm
Still rumbles. And again she almost
Smiles. Watt III *says another*
Voice. Und I und
II *I add. And so it*
Goes on. "The political one about
The two cats." Ja,
Das politische / *she repeats*
Ironically:

Conflict of Interests

I saw in Lohme
A white cat with
Blue eyes / in Liselund
A red green-eyed
Cat / and for a long
Long time was quite unable
To decide which I
Preferred.

And in the silence following
Vorzog / *echoes her resounding*
Refusal / even as much as to mention
Our workaday world of
The workaholic city: ruthless
Reification / buying and selling of
Souls / insatiable greed / arrogant power-
Mongering / consumption and de-
Fecation of innocent
Beauty / business – deutschmarks *– deadlines –*
Dollars – (mis)management – pounds – "Ja, das
Politische"*: all*
Conspicuous by their gaping
Absence:

Angel

Before I
Write my own untruths
In stone / or

Sow them in frozen
Earth:

Your house stands
On the brim of the world / I pass
Through its empty garden.
The window burns red /
I am as deathly pale
As fallen snow.

Voices

I will arise and go now / and go
To Gardskagi. At midnight
It's light there / and I hear
The sea attacking the coast.

Who are you / fragile voices / why go
About disguised as stags / who or what
Are you / you know no death.

Spring-Tide II

From tar-black sea the moon
Rises. You'd better
Get under cover / beloved
Heart. Before nostalgia
Starts whimpering its lost dream / of
Yore. The moon
My oblivion shines
Red. Cold
The frost that's fallen
Upon me. I long for
My childhood dream / of the beauty
Of the world / which lies
So wretchedly decaying / so
Ill.

And why should she not – as disregarded
Prophet – be disappointed? As dishonoured –
Impotent – irrelevant – outré –

Outsiders / why should we not
Indulge in anger – bitterness –
Cruelty – even
Guilt? After such knowledge / after
The usual keenness of Christians / to
Inform on their neighbours / (she
Unusually *confused the* Stasi *by*
Angrily confronting the
Beamter *on her tail / demanding*
To know what he'd like to know / or –
According to the file they gave her – remarking
"Well, aren't you badly disguised
Again today?") / after
The disappearances / the deaths / the
Dismissal / and, later, the
Revelations – whose brother, friend, colleague /
Including artistic colleague /
Informed on whom – and in no
Other Eastern bloc country / were there
So many duty-bound voluntary
Helpers – after such knowledge / such
Exclusion / what
Forgiveness? "Aber ist
Das eine Antwort?" *Is*
Such star-dwelling isolation / such
Withdrawal / any
Answer? The child is dead / will never
Be found. As Erlking's daughter / how
Could she ever
Find it

Easy

There was nothing that could
Detain me / no mainland kept
Me busy long. I always
Jumped aboard the last
Ship / as it was leaving
In September.

Fool's Song

Know how I guessed?
From the stone on my
Chest. Just heaved it
Into the heavens.

This unfooled audience – relieved
Not to be different / not
To be in her English shoes / in which
Fen-water sloshes – knowing
Enough / to empathize with exile / even
Imagining its romantic
Attractions / would truly love
To have her read
Them all again. But she ends with

Distance

Never again on the poor
Greensward shall glory
Lie as in childhood when still
The firs grew green and
Gleaming. Black
Knowledge bows my head.

Free Verses

I woke last night / knowing
I ought now to say farewell
To these verses. That's always how it is
After several years. They'll have to make their way
In the world. They can't be kept
Forever! here under cover.
Poor things. They'll have to go to town.
A few may be allowed to return
Later. But most will hang around elsewhere.
Who knows what will become of them. Before
They settle down.

And so she settles down / bowing
Her head / to signing a long
And patient queue / of first
Editions. Suspending
My insurgent disbelief / in
My own or international
Capitalism's future
Prosperity / I
Happily spend too much / observing
That Fr. Kirsch's tiny / and
Not particularly inspiring watercolours / which
I dutifully admire
As instructed / seem very
Expensive indeed. (A pity / I
Have sometimes thought / I gave up
Drawing!) Back
In the polished U-Bahn */ I inadvertently*
Step into a compartment / crowded
With refugees – strange-looking
Foreigners, at any rate – with battered
Suitcases / plastic bags / small
Children and cardboard boxes – wearing
Drab and ill-fitting clothes / speaking
Unrecognizable languages. A prim Bavarian
Couple / in matching Loden-
Mänteln */ though hopelessly*
Outnumbered / exchange disapproving
Glances. And though the wind in
The Englischer Garten */ howls*
In the naked tree-tops / whips
Up waves on even the tamed
Water of the complacent
Picturesque lake for paddle-
Boats / overfed ducks / and silly
Geese / she wrinkles her nose
At smells of unwashed shirts and
Garlic / he mutters an old / but
Explosive cliché / about the shortage
Of flats and work. The grass will be white
With driving snow / the park
Will be dark and deserted. And
Like many if not most
Bavarians / they will almost certainly
Be a generation or two away

From medieval, profoundly
Catholic, church- and village-
Oriented peasantry / blessed – as I have learned
To my chagrin – with a marked
Tendency / towards extreme
Toughness / both
Physical and
Emotional. Since the common
"Good" must be resolutely
Pursued by all / and since
To pursue it / one
May be assertive – if not
Aggressive – hard-headed, humourless and
Relentlessly efficient / they rather rarely
Apologize. A people such as
This people shall / surely! inherit
The earth. But it is not
A good thing to stand out. And I
Am consciously relieved / at Münchener
Freiheit / to flee the openly
Republican sentiments / of this well-dressed
Respectable couple / and of the well-dressed
Respectable couple / who
Have joined them: "It's hardly surprising
Now, is it? if we Germans get a bit
Upset: there really are too many
People who don't belong here. Well, it can't
Go on like this. So why not
Send them back where they came from?" Believers
In organized authority – like innumerable
Burghers across the civilized
Global village – and functioning best in
Groups / all members of which
Are entitled to mind the others'
Business / tame their children / raise
Their voice at irregularities / and
Conspire to assert the will
Of community / gang or gaggle /
Over the individual / they make excellent
Businessmen, policemen, soldiers,
Educators, priests, orchestral
Musicians / and will no more than
Tolerate – with either grudging
Admiration / envious

Curiosity / or barely concealed
Dislike – anyone or anything
Different / including Gastarbeiter, *refugees,*
Big-mouthed homosexual film-
Makers, individualists of any
Denomination, poets, eccentrics – and, yes, even
Englishmen – as I ruefully
Reflect / on entering our tenement
Of flats / and passing (did I
Forget to clean the staircase
This week?) the Hausmeister's *orderly*
Notice-board. Among such rules
And regimentations / idleness or
Unemployment / are
Taboo. Arriving home / reminded
Of my unrequited hunger / and
Urgent need for
A drink / I nevertheless attempt – am
Tempted again – to escape
From today as well as
Tomorrow / by opening
At random / one of my latest
Impotent – irrelevant – outré
Sources of darkly
Sparkling / slowly
Growing / difference:

The Chronicler

Welling from the softly sharpened quill /
Black ink-strokes / sparkling darkly.

A river of repetitions. And horror
Flows from the trembling hand. It wanders

By day and night in distress across the paper.
Nothing much of interest happens nowadays.

And so the hand grows weary of writing.

(A volume of translations by Margitt Lehbert of Sarah Kirsch's poetry up to but not including *Erlkönigs Tochter* has been published by Anvil Press Poetry under the title *Winter Music*, 1994. Further translations, by W Mulford and A Vivis, are to be found in *The Brontës' Hats* and "*T*", Reality Street Editions, Cambridge.)

Hans Werner Cohn

Translated by Frederick G Cohn and by the author

Poems from **Hans W Cohn**'s *collection* Mit allen fünf Sinnen *(1994) were translated by his brother* **F G Cohn** *for* MPT *9. The whole collection, translated by F G Cohn, has now been published by Menard Press (1999). The poems here are from* Gedichte *(Sigbert Mohn Verlag, Gutersloh, 1964).*

Again Winter

Again Winter. Again Winterwind: Against-wind.
Again to the grave in his windingsheet
the body of love so that it lives through to the spring
perhaps.

The twig not yet ready
again from the tree of hope
it broke off it broke

the broken twig sweeps
rootless and useless and sightless through lanes and drains in the
        winterwind.
Again in the wind
split the seams of pictures so cheap
flutter in tatters the songs in a hurry
fly away nocturnal birds so holy:
Jacob misses his hour.

Again against the wind
bent and blind words drag themselves
words without hosts
wander into their winter.

Curly from clouds
drops drowsiness
softly wintering on weary lashes
and snowing up the withered mouth
so that when the bridal time is nearing
again it greens in the wind of spring
perhaps.

[FGC]

About the Man who Sits in the Cellar

The man sits in the cellar
and fades away:
a sprouting potato in the corner.
His hands hang flabbily across the knees
the shoulders swallow the head.

Sometimes the woman
comes into the cellar
and combs his hair
and wipes his ears
takes his arm and pulls him
as if on a lead
into the parlour:
there her lady-friends sit around the table.
They say: how nice! and also: how clever!
For in daylight he does not look so bad,
the man,
and thoughts become rampant
in the cellar-air
and now he turns them out in front of the lady-friends,
the man.
At the end of the presentation the woman pulls the man
back into the cellar.

This is her hour.
True: he is looking forward to it
because a little light
gets through the velvet
of the curtains
in the parlour.
But: it is her hour.
His hour will come
his hour is coming
at night.
The woman lies in bed
but the man is awake.
His hour is coming.
His head shoots up
between the shoulders
and knocks against the ceiling
red and wild

in time with the heart.
The hands become tense
red and wild
and beat in time with the heart
against the cellar-door.

The woman lies in bed
bathed in fear
in fear.

[FGC]

Residences

Narrow is the room of his belief. Often
he can hardly breathe in it. Bare
are its walls. It is poorly
heated. From the window one does not
see much.

Sometimes somebody visits and talks
of other places, more roomy,
in the woods or by the lake.

Sometimes he has been invited
to such places. Then he can feel
the shine and also the warmth. Lost he
runs through the bright rooms. Is
a guest. An alien.

Then he returns again to his own narrow
room. It is the only residence
he can afford. Perhaps after all
one day he will be able to see something
from his window.

[FGC]

Not at Home

Not at home in the body
a helpless guest with the lovers
with the children
by hearsay only familiar with affections begetting and birth.

Not at home in the spirit
Cold in the church and among worshippers
without tongue
or with forged phrases: a nuisance.

But not without love
concerned
with these fields so distant from one's own penury.

　　[HWC]

Günter Kunert

Translated by Gerald Chapple

Günter Kunert *is, at seventy-one, one of the grand old men of German literature. A native Berliner who left East Germany in 1979, he has published over two dozen volumes of poetry and prose, of which the most recent are his memoirs,* Erwachsenenspiele *(Adult Games) and a collection of verse,* Nacht Vorstellung *(Late Show), both in 1999. 'Witchcraft, Texas Style' first appeared in* Warnung vor Spiegeln *(Watch out for Mirrors, 1970), and the other two poems here are from* Mein Golem *(My Golem, 1996).*

Gerald Chapple *teaches German and Comparative Literature at McMaster University in Hamilton, Ontario, and has been translating German and Austrian writers for twenty years. Apart from Kunert's poetry, his latest (co-)translation is Barbara Frischmuth's* Chasing after the Wind: Four Stories, *which was awarded an Austrian Government translation prize in 1996.*

Günter Kunert's poems: © Hauser Verlag, Munich.

Witchcraft, Texas Style

Hands turned into clumps
by magic fire from the sky.
Children, amazed, after they've healed,
hold their brand-new, their forever
useless fingers up to their eyes:
can't figure out what's
happened to us because of the big speeches
of the big grownups, children, and their abracadabra
in front of the mikes, where
a wrinkle-browed President
conjures up peace, children, and with a mournful
look a ghost called "Fer-reedum":
a modern-day Merlin,
richer than anybody, who can do anything
except for one small thing:
burned children stay branded.

Keep away from falling fire, the water
carrying conquerors along, and
the Magna Carta of Human Rights:
a belated draught from Jean Jacques's
guts.

In the Waiting Room

Wobbles in and gingerly
sits himself down. Forgotten now
the great enthusiasm at the awakening.
That a new hope likewise
rose up along with him.

Now he has a toothache
and demands his daily paper.
The world is one huge wound.
That's good for my sore tooth.
What would happen if it were resurrected
in the flesh all that dead flesh
in the newspaper photos.

The windows are fogged up now
with the thought-sweat of people waiting
because thought turns violent the moment
it spreads around like an infection.

What's that awful stink
they're thinking and rightly guess
the source to be our Mr Lazarus here
the next patient who once again is
getting preferential treatment.

"Mehr Licht"

His face turned to the wall
Goethe on his deathbed
You only hear the scratching
of his fingernails
the searching for the secret door-latch
to a futurity
which will be darker

as if I had been present

Bucolic Elegy IX

The gardener comes to know
death. Leaves are dying en masse
like unteachable hordes of people.
The foxglove ages grumpily
bowing low: where has all my beauty
gone to? Nature's
greenery reverts to rot.
The gardener suffers through each autumn,
allegorical Nature.
Beneath his soles the dried-out leaves complain
undiscerning: last lamenting sighs.
In the rain barrel floats
Ophelia, garbed
in graying fur.
Wherever the gardener looks: the coma
spreads itself out.
Who ever's going to re-awaken life?
The gardener knows how to wait and
thinks: this all comes back with time. Just
the gardener won't.

Hans Magnus Enzensberger

Translated by Michael Hamburger

Hans Magnus Enzensberger *was born in Bavaria in 1929 and grew up in Nazi Nuremberg. Generally considered the most important of contemporary German poets, he is a social and cultural critic and a political thinker whose satire has informed his poetry as well as his essays. His 1995 collection,* Kiosk *(translated by Michael Hamburger and published by Bloodaxe in 1997), is reviewed in this issue by Richard Dove.*

Michael Hamburger, *poet and doyen of translators from German, contributed translations of Günter Grass to* MPT 13; MPT 2 *(a bilingual issue) was devoted to his translations of unpublished poems by Franz Baermann Steiner. His translation of a poem by WG Sebald appears in this issue. The poems here are taken from* Leichter als Luft; Moralische Gedichte *(Suhrkamp, Frankfurt, 1999).*

Lighter than air

Poems don't carry
very much weight.
As long as the tennis ball rises
it is, or seems to me to be
lighter than air.

Helium in any case,
inspiration, this itch
inside our brains,
St Elmo's fire too
and natural numbers.

They weigh next to nothing,
not to speak of
the transcendental ones,
their upper-class cousins,
although they are numberless.

As far as I know, this holds
good for the radiation of magnets
which we do not see,
for most haloes
and all waltz tunes without exception.

Lighter than air,
like a grief forgotten
and the bluish smoke
of the finally last cigarette,
is our self, of course,

and, as far as I know,
the burnt offering's odour
so pleasing to the gods
always rises heavenward.
So does a Zeppelin.

A great many things, in any case,
remain in suspense.
Lightest of all perhaps
weighs that which remains of us
when we've gone underground.

John von Neumann (1903-1957)

Double chin, moonface, a slight waddling –
that must be a comedian
or a general agent for carpeting,
a bon-vivant of the Rotary Club.

But look out when Janesi from Budapest
begins to think!
Relentlessly under his cranium
the soft processor ticks,
a flicker runs through the data-bank
and like lightning it emits ballistic equations.

In three moves he's checkmated
Eichmann and Stalin: Göttingen–Cherbourg,
Cherbourg–New York, New York–Princeton.
By first-class carriage he left the lethal zone.

Four hours of sleep was all he needed,
a large dollop of whipped cream on his poppyseed strudel
and a few Swiss bank accounts.

Even someone who's never heard of him
(and that is most of us)

with a mouse in his hand sets in motion
his Schaltag algebra.
And as for Artificial Intelligence –
without his perhaps even today it would be
a changeling with no address.
Never mind whether it's a game of dice
or a hurricane,
a fruit machine or a firing range,
the chalk in his hand limps on behind –
so fast is his neural nexus.
Manically he jots down Hilbert spaces,
rings and ideal. Unrestricted
he operates with unrestricted operators.
The main thing is: *elegant solutions*
to set the planet dancing.

An ageing infant prodigy with an interface for the Secret Service.
Chugging the helicopters land on his lawn.
"Fat Man" on Nagasaki: pure mathematics.
War as a drug. *There's no such thing*
as a weapon too large. Always in a good mood
when lunching with admirals.
Really he is shy, and there are enigmas
in the face of which his black box fails.
Love, for instance,
stupidity, boredom.

Pessimism = sin against science.
Energy out of the tin, climate control, perpetual growth!
To convert Iceland into a tropical paradise –
no problem. The rest makes no difference.

Then the staff outing to another island,
in his double-breasted suit, with dark glasses: Bikini.
"Operation Turning-Point". The test was successful.
It took radiation cancer ten years
to turn off his synapses.

Equisetum

For the horsetail the facts are these:
it *was* much larger at one time,
a few hundred million years ago.

Devon, Perm, Keuper –
those were the days!

Later its dainty shoots
served Grandma, yours and mine,
to scour dirty pots.
Now it's not used any more,
only its ancestors, gouged
out of the deep, are fuel still.

Horsetail ignores us,
does not need us, discreetly proliferates.
In boggy roadside ditches
it waits, more simple than we are
and invincible thanks to that.
The measureless future calmly awaits
its glorious geometry.

Terminal B, Departure Lounge

Just behind the security lock
on the polished black granite
this feather, rust-brown, golden, snow-whitely-
tongued, leopard-flecked, brindled.
Lift it up, it weighs little,
don't be afraid to examine it!
Bustard? Partridge? Pheasant?
No flutter, no bird's cry.
Under the glass roof
only monitors and monotonous voices.
"Mr Buffon please come to the exit gate."

It will be a manual rocker arm,
the flags not quite symmetrical,
something fluffy at the spool
and at the dim end of the keel
the soul has its seat. How the light plays
with the iridescent colours
and how, when you scrutinize
your find more clearly, hook,
loop and feather rays so finely,
so microscopically interlace
that you're moved to tears!

But this much you can see with your naked eye,
that it's perfect,
the lost feather,
as behind the protective partition glass
on Bay 36 the noiselessly thrumming
jumbo jet you have missed.

Noises

Peace at last, now they're all sleeping,
the bellowing football fans,
rally bikers,
drunks, drug pushers.
Only very far off, invisible,
on the neon sky,
a rescue helicopter clacks.
But then you hear this dripping –
what can it be that drips there
and drips? A technical whirr
is inside the concrete, something fluid
feebly trickles, in your ear there's a crackle,
in your joints, softly the air
in your lungs hisses,
currents crackle in your hair,
ghostly, and the more you listen
the more distinctly you catch
frequencies from the beyond, it's enough
to drive you out of your wits!
You put your hands to your ears
in vain. But then, no sooner than
you've dropped your hands again –
listen! Nothing stirs any more,
anywhere. Nothingness stirs.
Panic stillness, silence.

Softer Tones

Always only increasing the dose,
that's quite wrong. Provisionally
leave most things aside –
not bad either: softer words,
less of a din in poetry
and in the consumer market.

Quite possibly it will come yet,
the blue hour, provisionally,
before the next deadly drop-out begins
to shoot into the crowd.

Fluffy things, adagio,
attentively, to the point of thoughtlessness
to touch upon something that yields,
the corner of a mouth or a moss.
Altogether, it's the slighter feelings
you can rely on most even now.

At the Hairdresser's *or* What's Important?

Read a few pages of Jean Paul in New Zealand –
a rare sort of pleasure,
but Adlestrop or Weybread
would have done just as well.

What speaks against shopping centres is this:
Did you notice the empty boxes
at the back entrance, piled up
for no purpose or use?

Boxes? What sort of boxes?

Whereas that little paw . . .

Paw? Is it paw you said?

. . . that black and white spotted cat's paw,
how at the kitchen door's chink it plucks, plucks:
that paw knows what it wants.

*Do you mean to tell me
there's nothing more important on your mind?*

Importance! Just to hear that word . . .
Can't you see that old man over there,
how he holds out his frothy head
to the nineteen-year-old girl in the green apron,
his eyes shut?
A fingertip sensation,

blonde and ephemeral –
that's it, and hardly
anything besides.

Identity Card

I is different
I is different from itself
I can't grasp it
I has to remain fleeting
be there absently
I the sleeper has to fight
I the saver has to spend lavishly
I unwittingly know what's what
I the embodiment of politeness
rages foams at the mouth curses
I the blabber gives away nothing
I the selfless begrudger
I the bloodthirsty peace-maker
I doesn't matter
On I you can rely
I lets down each and everyone
I composed to the point of indifference
has to care about everything
I the hopeless case
can't leave it alone
I battles on and on
I excuses itself
must soon be gone
I is different

WG Sebald

Translated by Michael Hamburger

WG Sebald *was born in Wertach in Bavaria, and studied in Freiburg and Switzerland. He settled permanently in England in 1970, and is Professor of Modern German Literature at the University of East Anglia. Two of his works of fiction have been translated into English:* The Emigrants *(Harvill, 1996)* and Vertigo *(Harvill, 1999). His remarkable and unclassifiable book* The Rings of Saturn *(translated by Michael Hulse; Harvill, 1998) shares a landscape and a mood with the poem here.*

Michael Hamburger's *translations of poems by Enzensberger appear in this issue.*

After Nature

When morning sets in,
the coolness of the night
moves out into the plumage
of fishes, when once more
the air's circumference
grows visible, then at times
I trust the quiet, resolve
to make a new start, an excursion
perhaps to a region of
camouflaged ornithologists.
Come, my daughter, come on, give
me your hand, we're leaving
the town, I'll show you the mill
twice each day set in motion by current,
a groaning miraculous construct
of wheels and belts
that carries water's power
right into stone,
right into trickling dust
and into the bodies of spiders.
The miller is friendly,
has clean white paws,
tells us all kinds of lore
to do with the story of flour.
A century ago here Edward Fitzgerald,
the translator of Omar Khayyam,
vanished. At an advanced age

one day he boarded his boat,
sailed off with his top hat
tied on, into the North Sea
and was never seen again.
A great enigma, my child, look,
here are eleven barrows
for the dead and in the sixth
the impress of a ship long gone
with forty oars, the grave of
Raedwald of Sutton Hoo.
Merovingian coins, Swedish
weaponry, Byzantine silver
the king took on his voyage
and his warriors even now
on this sandy strip keep their weapons
hidden in grassy bunkers
behind earthworks, barbed wire
and pine plantations, one great
arsenal as far as your eye can see,
and nothing else but this sky,
the gorse scrub now and then,
a capacious old people's home,
a prison or mental hospital,
an institution for juvenile delinquents.
In orange jackets you see
the inmates labour
lined up across the moor.
Behind that the end of the world,
the five cold houses of the place called Shingle Street.
Inconsolable a woman
stands at the window, a children's swing
rusts in the wind, a lonely
spy sits in his dormobile
in the dunes, his radio's earphones
clipped on. No, here we can
write no postcards, can't even get out
of the car. Tell me, child,
is your heart heavy as
mine is, year after year
a pebble bank raised
by the waves of the sea
all the way to the North,
every stone a dead soul
and this sky so grey.

So unremittingly grey
and low
as no sky I have seen
anywhere else.
Along the horizon
freighters cross over
into another age
measured by the ticking
of geigers in the power station
at Sizewell, where slowly
they destroy the nucleus
of the metal. Whispering
madness on the heathland
of Suffolk. Is this
the promis'd end? Oh,
you are men of stones.
What's dead remains
dead. From loving
comes life. I don't know
who's telling me what, how,
where or when? Is love
nothing, then, now, or all?
Water? Fire? Good?
Evil? Life? Death?

Michael Hamburger writes: The lines translated here constitute Section 6, Part III of WG Sebald's poem 'Nach der Natur', published in 1988 before the unclassifiable prose books that won him his international readership and acclaim. A straight translation of the title, 'After Nature', renders the terrible ambiguity which Sebald must have intended. 'Post-nature', like 'post-Modernist', is likely to become part of the stock of political-cum-cultural correctness, as indicated in a recent prominent anthology of twentieth-century verse.

Readers of the prose books will recognise the questing and questioning mobility that distinguishes Sebald's writing, the connections he makes between seemingly disparate phenomena and orders of experience, his peculiar leaps from the immediately observed to historical enquiry and an imaginative freedom usually expected only of fiction. If they are struck by the gloom of Sebald's response to East Anglian impressions here, the ambiguity of the title is one clue to it. Another is that he was born in an alpine region of Germany, shortly before the end of the war, and a region so remote from post-natural developments that it was spared the destruction by aerial bombardment that is the theme of Sebald's most recent prose book, not yet available in English. A third, perhaps, that, unlike more spectacular regions, East Anglian landscapes and seascapes grow on one, as I can testify as a fellow immigrant to the region. Although Sebald's vision – in *The Rings of Saturn* also – is marked by a melancholia induced less by his voluntary displacement than by a deep concern with the horrors and upheavals of the century now ending, the East Anglia of the prose books is more differentiated than that of the poem – not least because it draws on longer and wider familiarity, not the single excursion that assumes its full significance only in the context of the other landscapes, including an American one, evoked in the whole long poem.

One thing that drew me to this extract was that my first visit to East Anglia was an even stranger one: on a military exercise in wartime – probably 1944, the year of Sebald's birth – so secret that I discovered only later that it took place in West Suffolk. On this exercise, because of my knowledge of German, my part was to impersonate a German soldier to be taken prisoner and interrogated by Polish troops involved in it. This surreal experience left impressions even more sinister and absurd than any of Sebald's. No wonder that for holidays in later years I chose the Cornish and Welsh coasts, with their defiantly rocky cliffs and the rock-pools teeming with marine life I had explored ever since my childhood – until we moved to East Suffolk, slowly learning to love a bleaker sea, not always as grey as that of Sebald's poem, and be content with the undulations of land that had seemed flat at first. This became one of many links to Max Sebald, his person and his work. In our rare meetings and correspondence, just as in his texts, everything comes to hang together.

This translation and its accompanying note
first appeared in the programme for the
1999 Aldeburgh Festival of Music and the Arts.

Ulla Hahn

Translated by Oliver Grannis

Ulla Hahn *was born in 1946 in Germany, where she still lives and works. Her first collection of poems was widely acclaimed when it appeared in 1981, and with the publication of six additional volumes since then, she is now considered to be among the finest lyric poets in the country. In addition to her own extensive writings – poetry, essays and a novel – she has done a great deal to bring the work of other poets to the attention of the public, editing a collection of poems by the great German poet, Gertrud Kolmar, and publishing two anthologies. Ulla Hahn has a doctorate in literature. She worked for a number of years as a radio editor, has taught at several German universities and is the recipient of many prestigious literary prizes.*

Oliver Grannis *writes and translates poetry. He is professor emeritus for English language and linguistics at the University of Osnabrück.*

from **Galileo und zwei Frauen**, *1997.*

The Ballad of Galileo and Two Women

The job, husband, child, writing, everything
Neatly together: it doesn't work anymore.
Puts out one cigarette and lights
The next. Another glass of wine.

We're sitting in Da capo. The first
Telescope showed the jagged edges
Of the moon – an unappealing pattern
Full of peaks and gaps. Abandoned

That's what he'll be my friend says
She'll leave him and jabs out in front of her
With her fork. To be free. I too
Have left a man. The sun

Not the earth at the centre. He wept.
And I couldn't touch him anymore. Chianti
Saltimbocca a salad. Golden light through
Highset windowpanes. Such young arms

The young girl at the next table has
Around a young man. Does a woman like my friend
Have one arm too many one too few? Are
We then monsters? Are we insatiable?

The priests opposed to Galileo refused
To look through the telescope, justified themselves
With God, the Ptolemaists. Telescopes were
Unknown there. The lover's presence. Our house

Milk bottles at the door. The earth a slice
Of black bread with heather honey. Can you
Pick up our child? Bring the paper with you.
That and that other matter – that with

The third arm. At the desk. Alone
With the unproven. Obsessed, lost in thought
Galileo stared into the darkness. Jupiter has
Four moons. He threw the warnings to the wind.

When he was old blind silent a student
Asked him if he had really recanted. Yes
He said. They showed me the tongs and
My blood ran cold for fear. I knew

A woman who at forty gave up playing
The piano: pills shock treatment finally into
The water; after five children her daughter took up
Painting. Cancer and already dead at fifty. And I then

Am *her* daughter. My body is afraid. The sun not
The earth at the centre: thus Galileo at the end.
And, Jupiter has three moons. This as prisoner
In dungeon candlelight and quickly failing

Sight. Bill, please. And it does
Move indeed: it would have been nice
If that sentence had really been his. Outside
In the heavens – the gentle moon. No

Trace of jagged edges.
Entirely smooth entirely
Soft round and perfect.

For Dorian Gray

The heart of those last warm days the sky
breaking up thin strips of light in the north
and all those lovely dead white upon white
the full moon coming up among the birches
How very much we miss the unbearable
we then called Heat
rustling of snakes swallows
flown away like words
from an unwell mind.

Hypothetical Sonnet

Were we to breathe more deeply slowly
softly tread and gently turn our eyes
to one another quietly speak and
seldom, we would live forever

not just a bit forever but much
more like the sea perhaps or even
seaborn words and sentences
or this very afternoon today

when we bring each other to forget
whatever happens wherever
would last let's say three weeks or four

which then again some
twofold threefold years
at least – just now.

Untitled (*from* 'In fremden Häusern')

Lived only in strange houses
and in words. Fear
something could belong to me alone
No pictures hung on walls
no oven round the fire
Keep time fluid Sleep in between
my head on my suitcase
full of lifsfrgmnts.

Muse Asleep

None of these books now being printed
will she ever be able to read
nor will she ever know again
the consolation of the trees
not even the tips of the buds nor
that lovely moment without pain
They've hardened all to stone
to lie one over the other on her breast
and her bit of life is more and more
this heavy harshness these hard core
obscenities of force and degradation.

If only there weren't so much
about her still honey and golden   the thin peaked face
under a kerchief   the face of a little muse
Why
is she being pulled out of life like this
a bad apple from the middle of the crate? My hate's
an ill-fitting wedding ring without a finger

Morning   All night I've been with her
by her high bed
She liked so much to play
new games new luck pokering
with herself   with others   the way she wanted
by her own rules   Everything goes   and now
everything's going the way life wants and
life's own rules are law rejecting everything
certain   absolutely everything   Never again
a chance to choose this thing or another
not now nor soon
not even between coffee or tea   The morning
staff arrives   She's sleeping   I'll be able
to leave   I can go   I can
even walk on water as long as the ice holds
or stay here in the room already warming
in the February sun.

from **Spielende**, *1983.*

Tidying Up

Quietly so very quietly
you dressed then sighed
quite quietly tenderly
again you lied

Then quietly so quietly
you closed the door and stole
away and quietly you stopped
to tidy up your quiet soul.

from **Herz über Kopf**, *1981.*

Respectable Sonnet

So why not write a respectable sonnet   – St.H.

Come bite me right and bite right in again
and leave off merely nibbling. Here's where
it's good, and here, and you know where, yes, there,
and take my measure mouth to mouth. Paint then

considering these eyes, rings around
them, let me hide behind beneath my hand,
then spring to yours. Pleasure me in sixes and
in sevens. I scream I know no sound.

Stay with me. Wait. I'll come again,
back to myself, to you, and once more tell
you too, I'll be your lovely old refrain.

Rub rings of sunshine into belly's shell
so that the warmth remain.
Then keep my eyelids open, my lips as well.

Louise Labé

Translated by Timothy Ades

Louise Labé, *c.1524–1556, was the leading woman poet of the French Renaissance. 'La belle cordière de Lyon' (her husband was a ropemaker, like her father) was a poet of the most delicate wit. She left 24 Sonnets, three Elegies and the* Debate of Folly and Love, *an elaborate prose work. She also inspired 24* Hommages, *or tributes to herself, which appeared in her lifetime: some of them are by the best French poets of the day. Her sonnets have been recreated in English at least five times, but no other version of the Elegies is known to this translator. She is said to have fought at the battle of Perpignan, disguised as a knight, but this may be just another of the rumours that accrued to her name.*

Timothy Ades, *born in 1941, learnt classical verse composition at school, read Mods & Greats at Oxford and studied international business management. His 33 Sonnets of Jean Cassou were placed equal first in the BCLA/BCLT Prize, 1996. His version of* Homer in Cuernavaca *by Alfonso Reyes is forthcoming. From German he has translated works by Hans Arp, Ricarda Huch and Brecht. His work from French includes Hugo's* Booz Endormi *and other (lipogrammatic) poems in* MPT 8, *where some of the Cassou sonnets first appeared.*

Sonnet XXIV

Ladies, reproach not my amours:
If I for burning firebrands languish,
Feel pricks and pangs and biting anguish,
If I with weeping waste my hours,

Do not abuse me with your blame.
If I have erred, the pains are pressing;
Make not their rigours more distressing:
Think that if Cupid but take aim,

Never your Vulcan-heat excusing,
Never Adonis' charms accusing,
Cupid can swell your tender yearning,

Having not even my occasion,
Yet knowing stranger, stronger passion.
Then guard ye well 'gainst fortune's turning.

Sonnet XIV

As long as I can sit with streaming eyes
And want to spend another hour with you;
As long as I can stifle sobs and sighs
And use my voice to get a message through;

As long as I've a hand can tune the strings
Of my guitar, to sing a song of you;
As long as I've no heart for other things
But only want to get the hang of you:

There's no way I'll be lying down to die.
No, but the day I feel my eyes run dry,
My voice crack up, my hand with zero power,

My heart, too close to earth, no longer giving
Signals that lovers give: then, I'll quit living . . .
Death, turn my daylight black, that very hour!

Elegy I

When Love, who conquers Gods and men,
Had set my poor heart blazing; when
He torched in fury most unkind
My blood and courage, bones and mind;
I lacked the power to complain,
Express my suffering and pain.
Apollo of the laurel-tree
Hadn't yet set my verses free;
But now his sacred rage inspires,
And fills my breast with bold desires:
He has me sing, not Jove nor Mars,
Not thunder, nor the cruel wars
That shake, at will, the universe:
The lyre he gave me sang the verse
Of Lesbian Sappho's ancient love,
And now to mine its strings shall move.
Sweeten my voice, sweet curving bow!
With so much grieving it might grow
Bitter, or break, with all the pains,
Misfortunes, setbacks, sorrows, strains.
Damp down the fires by which my tender

Heart was once toasted to a cinder:
For now I feel the memory
That brings a sad tear to my eye:
I seem to feel the first alarms
I had of Love; I see the arms
He used for his assault on me.
It was my eyes that lavishly
Shot looks at those who shot, just so,
At me, unshielded from my bow.
Those ogling glances doomed my eyes,
Made me a case for Nemesis.
I teased: I saw one man desire,
Another perish in the fire;
I saw so many sprinkled tears,
Such reckless waste of sighs and prayers,
I didn't notice, suddenly,
The same fate overtaking me.
So murderously was I gored
That, even now, I'm still not cured,
And cannot but repeat again
And re-create my lived-through pain,
With new sad songs. I ask you, ladies,
To sigh along with me. Dear readers!
It's possible one day I'll do
The same thing back, assisting you
To mourn your troubles and your pain
And all the time you've spent, in vain.
Be your heart never so severe,
Love can effect a conquest here;
The more you've been obtusely brave,
The worse he'll treat you, as his slave.
Do not assume it's right to blame
The ladies Cupid sets aflame.
Many with haughty fantasies
Have suffered love's indignities:
Pride, pedigree and pulchritude
Could not avert their servitude
To ruthless Love: the best are found
Suddenly, definitely, downed.
The famous queen Semiramis
Flattened as if with pyramids
The sable hosts of Ethiopia;
Her swordplay spilled a cornucopia
Of brave men's blood. The flow was ample,

Setting her team a fine example.
She, still desiring to pursue,
Attack her neighbours, and subdue,
Found Love, who pressed and crushed her so,
She let her swords and statutes go.
Didn't her royal circumstance
Deserve a less malign mischance?
She lost her heart: she loved her son!
O martial queen of Babylon,
What happened to that sword and shield
That forced your bravest foe to yield?
Where is the warlike helm and crest
That held your golden locks compressed?
Where is that blade and that cuirass
That broke the foeman's neck of brass?
Where have they fled, the chargers furious
That pulled your chariot, when victorious?
Soon as you smashed the feeble foe,
Your manly heart went soft as dough:
And war's delights no longer touch;
You merely languish, on a couch.
You quit the bitterness of war
And found the sweet, soft joys once more:
Thus from yourself by Love estranged,
You're to another person changed.
So, anyone who hears my cries
In Love's constriction, don't despise
My sorry dirge: for Love, with brief
Delay, may bring you equal grief.
I knew a lady who was cold
To Love, when young; when she was old,
She burned, lamenting piteously
The pangs of late-life agony.
With paints and scented sprays she'd try
Repeatedly to beautify
And smooth the furrows of the plough
That age had etched across her brow;
On her grey locks she chose to wear
A poorly-grafted piece of hair.
The more she gaily rouged and creamed,
The less her lover-boy esteemed:
He fled without a thought, for she
Looked hideous: he felt shame to be
Her fancy. So the poor old bat

Got her comeuppance, tit for tat.
Once hopelessly pursued by many,
She loves, but is not loved by any.
So Love contrives, and takes delight,
That all our wants are opposite.
One, whom a lady loves, loves not;
Another, who's not loved, is hot,
And obstinately will maintain
His rigid strength, though hope is vain.

Elegy II

As the slave longs for liberty,
for haven's calm the ship at sea,
just so, as days go by, I yearn,
my darling, for your safe return.
That's been the goal of all my pain:
the joy of seeing you again;
but, thwarted by the long delay,
my yearning's turning to dismay.
Cruel! Who made you swear to come
back soon, in your first letter home?
Faithless already? Can I be
so little in your memory?
How can you dare to be untrue
to one who's been so true to you?
Now possibly beside the Po,
a two-horned river, as we know,
your courage flares with some new flame:
you've swapped me for another dame,
and fickle and forgetful, you
betray the trust that was my due.
If so, and if your loyalty
has gone, likewise your decency,
I shouldn't be surprised if you
by now have lost all pity too.
How pensive and how full of fear
my lovestruck heart, left lonely here!
Seeing what our love used to be,
you cannot have deserted me:
again I pledge your faith and, yes,
I value your trustworthiness
as more than human. Are you ill,

perhaps, detained against your will,
somewhere remote? I doubt it, seeing
I've prayed so much for your well-being:
the gods would be brute beasts, if they
allowed disease to come your way;
although your fickle waywardness
deserves some punitive redress.
The One enthroned above the sky
couldn't, I think, this much deny:
hearing me cry and weep and pray
for you, He'd turn His wrath away.
I've always lived by His behest;
only this one vice I'll attest:
not Him, but you, I've oft adored
– Love forced me to it – as my Lord.
Twice now the moon's closed horn to horn
since the due date of your return,
and all this time, my love, I've still
no news of you, for good or ill.
Anyway, if you're weak with love
in foreign parts, and so can't move,
I do know this: your latest flame
will hardly have the kind of fame
for beauty, virtue, grace, and wit
that many who've looked into it
ascribe (I think they're wrong) to me.
But who can guard celebrity?
Not just in France am I acclaimed,
and, much beyond my wishes, famed:
but in the land between the seas
and Pyrenees and Hercules;
and where the wide Rhine rolls his sand;
and where you rove, that lovely land:
they've heard (I quite believe your story)
the wise and witty grant me glory.
Taste what so many men desire:
inhabit, where the rest aspire:
you'll find none better anywhere.
I don't say others aren't more fair,
but I shall love you more than these,
your honour I shall more increase.
Many great Lords pursue my love,
prepared to please me and to serve:
contests and jousts they undertake,

wear splendid favours for my sake.
I care so little, I ignore it,
and do not even thank them for it.
You are my only good and ill;
with you I've all, without you, nil:
I've nothing that can please my mind,
and there's no pleasure I can find:
I'm wearied, far from being pleased:
by tears and sorrows I am seized:
and so discomforted am I,
a thousand times I want to die.
So while you're far away, my lover,
not life, but death by love, I suffer:
ten thousand times a day I'm slain;
two months I've lingered in this pain.
So come back quickly, if you'd give
a fig to see me while I live;
and if, before you make it, death
has stilled this loving soul's last breath,
come back in black for just a day
to see my coffin put away.
Then on white marble, if God grants a
last prayer, be inscribed this stanza:

I LIVED AND FLAMED, LOVE , IN YOUR FIRES:
I LANGUISHED AND I BURNT AWAY.
IN MY HOT ASHES THEY HOLD SWAY,
UNLESS YOU QUENCH THEM WITH YOUR TEARS.

Elegy III

Ladies of Lyons, when you read
my querulous and lovesick screed
and hear me sing these wretched songs
of troubles, tears, regrets and wrongs,
don't censure my naïvety,
mistakes, and youthful idiocy.
Mistakes? But who beneath the skies
can claim exemption from all vice?
Some, discontented with their lot,
want what the folks next door have got;
some, straining after peace on earth,
encourage war for all they're worth;

some, thinking poverty a vice,
render to Gold their sacrifice;
some swear oaths falsely, and deceive
whoever's minded to believe;
others with lizard-tongues tell lies,
spreading canards and calumnies.
The ruling planets round my cot
decreed a less unhappy lot:
I don't go green-eyed if I see
next door get wetter rain than me;
I don't start brawls among good friends,
or work towards nefarious ends;
to lie, to cheat, to be two-faced,
to vilify, is not my taste;
but if I've any fault at all,
it's Love who is responsible.
He trapped me! I was green and tender,
and busy with a grand agenda
for mind and body, long and testing,
which he soon made uninteresting.
In mastery of needlecraft
I would have challenged and surpassed
that famed, accomplished, foolish spinster
who made Athene weave against her.
I put my martial skills on view:
I couched my lance, the quintain flew!
At the hot lists I did the deed
and spurred and swerved the noble steed
like Bradamante or proud Marphise,
and could have passed for one of these.
What then? Love could not bear to see
my love of war and artistry.
To put new worries in my head,
he smiled, and this is what he said:

"Lady of Lyons! Do you aspire,
with these pursuits, to dodge my fire?
You won't. I've conquered Deities
of hell below, of sea and skies:
d'ye think I can't make earthlings see
that nothing can escape from me?
All those who glory in their own
prowess, I quickly strike them down.
You trust in War, quite unashamed,

and he is praised, and I am blamed:
you can't go on, as you will see,
revering him, resisting me."
He spoke; hot rage suffused his face;
he drew an arrow from its case
and with full force, not aiming wide,
discharged it at my tender hide,
a rig too frail to guard the heart
from the all-conquering marksman's dart.
The breach is made, and in Love goes:
he quickly banishes repose
and gives no end of trouble, keeping
myself from drinking, eating, sleeping.
With sun and shade I'm not concerned:
love fires my courage, and I'm burned;
love casts me in a strange disguise,
a self I cannot recognise.
I wasn't sixteen winters old
when all these troubles first took hold:
and here's the thirteenth summer season
that Love has had me in his prison.
Now Time dries up the springs that flow,
lays Pyramids and Sphinxes low;
brave Colosseum and treasured town
he strikes inexorably down.
What if Love's fire is brightly lit?
Time likes to make an end of it.
And yet, in me, that fire augments
with time, and more and more torments.
Paris admired a Cretan maid,
but in two shakes his love decayed;
Jason, who thought Medea was neat,
soon turned her out into the street.
Ladies who love like these should earn
love and affection in their turn.
These men were loved, and yet they quit:
I'm unloved: I should tire of it,
and ask you, Love, for your consent
to terminate my punishment.
Don't make me weigh what Death can do:
I'd find Death more benign than you.
My darling makes me laugh and cry
like no-one else, and sigh, and sigh:
I'm his, all his: so, Love, if you

are keen for me to see it through,
raise in his heart, blood, bones, a flame
hotter than mine, or just the same.
I'll find your burden much less bother
when I can share it with another.

Remy Belleau and Etienne Jodelle

Translated by Geoffrey Brock

Remy Belleau *(1528-1577) was a member of the group of seven poets known as the Pléiade, of whom Ronsard and Du Bellay are the best known. Ronsard called Belleau 'the painter of nature', but the pastoral landscape of his* La Bergerie *is also, in the classical tradition, a background to reflections on love.*

Etienne Jodelle *(1532-1573), another member of the Pléiade, is best known as a dramatist whose work is a forerunner of the French classical theatre, but he also wrote several volumes of lyrical poetry (*Amours, Sonnets, Odes*).*

Geoffrey Brock *has had poems published in* New England Review, Gettysburg Review, Hudson Review *and* Southern Review. *In 1996 he won the Ezra Pound Translation Prize, and in 1998 he was awarded the Raiziss/ de Palchi Translation Fellowship of the Academy of American Poets. His translations of poems by Pavese appeared in* MPT *11.*

Remy Belleau

from **La Première Journée de la Bergerie**

Sonnet

While you with learned, kind and lovely hand
Pluck nimbly at the stems of fragrant flowers
In fields enamelled with a thousand colours
By the sacred work of the immortal band:

Take care that Love, veiled in the bright attire
Of some fresh flower, doesn't air his ardour
And, rather than appease your heart's disorder,
Compound it with a well-aimed shaft of fire.

Guileless Europa, gathering blooms like you,
Was overcome by Love, Persephone too –
One a king's daughter and the other a goddess.

All it would take is a quick breath of breeze
On a red coal to give rise to a blaze
Of which you would no longer be the mistress.

Etienne Jodelle

from **Les Amours (Loves)**

II

Pride of the stars, the woods, and Acheron,
Diana presides over high and middle and low,
Enlightening, hunting, and apportioning woe
As she drives her horses, hounds, and Furies on.

Such is the lustre, the thrill, the fear beneath
Your clear and swift and homicidal splendour
That Jupiter thinks less of his bolts of thunder,
Apollo less of his bow, and Pluto less of death.

Your beauty, with its glare and snares and horror,
Leaves the heart dazzled, captive, bound like a martyr;
Shine on me, seize me, keep me – ah, but do not repel

With your blazing torch, your meshes, your barricades;
Luna, Diana, Hecate, in heaven, on earth, in hell,
You grace, harass, and scourge our gods, us, and our shades.

X

Whether the sun with its splendid clarities
Gleams down on us, or whether the night's gloom
Blots it out, and with its shadowy claim
Blackens again the round vault of the skies;

Whether at last sleep seeps into my eyes
Or I lie awake chasing my curse's name,
I can no longer escape or stall for time
Or halt the tiresome course of my disease.

It's my bad luck to be forever chased
By cruel fortune, to be always thrashed –
And each day sees my suffering renewed.

But if these passions, which keep my soul in chains,
Do not assuage the misery of my days,
Then come, death, come and finish me for good.

XXI

I live and yet I die; my heart, the lord
Of these parts, governs poorly from afar:
Please, if you care that I complete my share
Of days, return my heart – or give me yours.

Thus you'll restore me to myself, and so
Restore yourself as well: passions that tether
One lover now will then link two together –
Or else your stricture strike a double blow.

You'll lose us both: first me, who loves too well,
Then you, who loving nothing will loathe yourself.
And if someday someone chooses to reprove

The two of us, me for my glut of esteem
And you for yours of hate, your crime will seem
More grave, since hatred's even worse than love.

from Contr'Amours (Counter Loves)

II

O you who have the head of Jove
For father and mother, who as you please
Can wage a war or keep the peace,
If I be yours and praise you alone

And if I distress for you the goddess
Who bore false Love, he whose arrows
Of peace and war, charms and sorrows,
Are plunging your poet into madness,

Then come, come help avenge your suitor.
Bring me the writhing locks of the Gorgons,
Squeeze the filthy paunch of your dragons,

Get me so drunk on Stygian water
That I puke such ordure on the lady
As she hoards in her soul and body.

Tristan Corbière

Translated by Christopher Pilling

Tristan Corbière *was born in 1845 in Brittany, the son of a sailor who was also a novelist. Always in poor health, Corbière managed to fill his short life (he died in 1875) with travels, practical jokes, irony and poetry. His collection of quirky, wholly original and frequently moving poems,* Les Amours jaunes (1873), *was published at his own expense; in 1883 Verlaine rescued him from almost certain oblivion by including him in* Les Poètes maudits, *along with Rimbaud and Mallarmé.*

Christopher Pilling's *translation of* Les Amours jaunes (These Jaundiced Loves) *was published in 1995 by Peterloo Poets.*

Christopher Pilling writes: Apart from the two couplets, the latter written in the copy of *Les Amours Jaunes* for Le Gad, Tristan's friend and favourite restaurateur in Roscoff, the following poems were found handwritten in his own copy and must date from 1873 or '74.

Paris by day

See the large red copper disc emblazon the sky,
Enormous saucepan in which the Good Lord above
Brings manna to the boil: left-overs, still called Try-
The-Chef's-Special, steeped in sweat and peppered with love.

Packed round a brazier the Dossers are milling,
You can vaguely hear their rancid flesh start to burn;
The boozers are there too, tankards up for filling;
One down-and-out shivers as he waits his turn.

You think it's the sun that's frying for young and old
These seething greasy meat-scraps, drenched in floods of gold?
No, it's pigswill for us that the heavens let fall.

While they stand in sunbeams, we've our backs to the wall,
Ours the pitch-pot going cold – here it isn't sunny! –
Our very substance is a bladder full of gall.

Christ, I'd rather have that than their pot of honey.

Paris by Night

> It's not a city, it's a world.

– It's the sea: – dead calm – The Spring tide has felt bound,
With a distant rumbling, to withdraw its sway.
Its waves will return, rolling themselves in their sound –
– Can you hear the crabs of night scratching away. . .

– It's the dried-up Styx: Rag 'n bone Diogenes,
Lantern in hand, wanders down it; he never squirms
But it's the black gutter where depraved poets please
To cast their lines, their hollow skulls the cans for worms.

– It's the wheat-field: Hideous harpies swirl and swoop
On what's impure, gleaning shreds of lint caked in pus.
The alley cat, on the watch for rats, flees the troop
Of Shit-creek's sons, harvesters of night's detritus.

– It's death: Here lieth the police – And love, upstairs,
Taking a siesta, sucks a heavy arm's meat
Where an old love-bite's left its blotch – Love is for pairs –
The hour is solitary – Listen: . . . dreams drag their feet . . .

– It's life: Listen: the spring water is up for air,
Singing its everlasting song, that seems to slide
Over a sea-god's slimy head, and his stretched bare
Green limbs on the bed of the Morgue . . . Eyes open wide!

Pierrot, be Hanged *(Pierrot pendu)*

I

Woman is a pill, a lily
Not to be gilded any more,
Your lyre, an implement that's silly
(. . . . .)

II

The comedy's over, a has-been,
Off to the Morgue with your Loves! such Likes!
Let's halt it, the worn-out machine
Of our days, when twelve o'clock strikes.

III

Just leave a talisman, a braid
Of hemp for that sweetheart of yours.
She was the gallery and stayed
To admire the show, for all its flaws.

IV

It'll be a comfort, albeit Dutch
– A last slip-knot in the halter –
In a fortnight's time it will touch
A stiff-collar whose love won't falter.

V

Let her trumpet it, the strumpet:
It's chaste too. Let her rattle, she's tight
In the throat, too stingy to hump it;
And let her walk the streets at night.

(Dedication)

Both of us are skilled, Le Gad, in the poisonous arts.
You poison people's stomachs, and I their hearts!

[*Translation of the dedication in Le Gad's copy of* LES AMOURS JAUNES.]

Couplet

I've been robbed, you know . . . – You haven't! Oh no, good grief!
– They've pinched my poems. – I *am* sorry . . . for the thief!

(Me your love . . .)

Me your love? – Never! – It was all put on, an act.
For my pure-chance disguise, I've Harlequin to thank:
The flaking smile that was making your plaster crack,
The drop of sweat that your excellent make-up drank.

My tongue was pasty with that acrid stickiness;
Laughingly we had our share of the black mascara
Which gave your eyes a false mother-of-pearl aura,
And your albino lashes a thistly prickliness.

Like your cheroots, I've smudged your rosy lips' lipstick
By foolishly licking off its red-currant slick
But your mouth is still laughing – it has never bled.

The penalty for kissing on stage is a pound per kiss . . .
Put your face back on, doll yourself up, brazen Miss
Jezebel, I tell you candidly, I loved that red.

Time for Bed
(smiling sweetly)

Pleasure was so hard for you, but evil's easy –
　　Let it thrive and come to a head.
It's no go the Muse, she's a death-mask and wheezy;
　　One goes off alone to be dead –

Your sheet knows your come and your handkerchief your snot;
　　Sing up, but do not bite the dust
By taking to the streets with your little begging pot
　　For a pittance of love or disgust.

You'll have a sleep: for troubled waters that's the oil;
Patient Death though is playing with your mortal coil,
　　Skinny-cat-with-a-mouse style;

Her velvet paw fondles you and throws you. Treasure
Such paroxysms – they're another sensual pleasure:
　　Twist your mouth, foam at the lips . . . and smile.

Arthur Rimbaud / Paul Valéry

Translated by James Kirkup

James Kirkup *was the featured translator in* MPT 11. *His translations of Rainer Franz Teuschl appeared in* MPT 5, *versions of Arabo-Andalusian poems, and a review article on* haiku, *in* MPT 6, *and of Apollinaire and Jacques Roubaud in* MPT 8. *Most recently, he contributed to the Pushkin Portfolio in* MPT 15, *which also includes his versions of Bertolucci.*

James Kirkup writes: I have often noticed that Japanese poets, when translating *haiku* into English, compose what is virtually a new poem, while preserving the theme and the spirit of the original. I have adopted this method in making a translation of Rimbaud's sonnet 'Voyelles', regular in form. Rimbaud's five vowels are given in the first line, with their colours: "A black, E white, I red, U green, O blue..." But I saw that these were not the only colours in the poem, which contains repetitions of "black", "white", but also new colours: purple, viridian and violet – ten colours altogether, though only eight if we omit the repetitions.

The rhyming of my translation is irregular, and I used my favourite form of the sonnet, two verses of seven lines each. I introduce fifteen different colours, none of which reflects Rimbaud's rainbow. I added a sixth vowel, "Y", which can be used as both a consonant and a vowel.

On the Sonnet of the Vowels: Homage to Rimbaud

A crimson, August, pavilion of blood,
summer fanfares, fading in eloquence
of E – a bitter orange solitude
in castled autumn's golden decadence
midwinter's invalid I, pale lemon.
Then green exclamatory O of spring –
emerald garlands of snow and blossom.

Ultramarine and azure seasons bring
blue U back into June – deep sapphire mists
ghosting the sleepless lamplight's rosy rains
to deepen dawn's faint lilac-tinted panes
in liquid violet of sombre Y –
symbol of symmetry and ancient trysts,
midnight groves, mystic indigo July.

It will be noticed that the colours carry us through all the seasons, from August through autumn, winter, spring and back into summer with June and July: a calendar of colours.

My version of 'D' from Valéry's *Alphabet* is another example. *Alphabet* is a series of twenty-two prose poems, illustrating ornamental capital letters – the illustrations are Valéry's own. I have not translated 'D' as a prose poem, but as a sequence of Japanese *tanka* in the strict traditional form: a verse of five lines of 5,7,5,7 and 7 syllables. It is an inspired and inspiring form, which works with the translator in a strange way that often suggests *le mot juste*.

D

Within the pure and
brilliant sarcophagus
how calm the water –
warm, marrying completely
the outlines of the body!

Free, light, the body,
naked, reposed, disposed
and in perfect peace.
All is ease in the fluid
where the lissom legs are both

as alive as arms, where
man deposits his stature,
flows full-length until
his height takes another form;
he stretches himself to reach

the extremity
of his unwinding; he feels
one with a sense of
his ability to let
himself be fully released.

Delightfully, he
transposes his fulcrums of
balance: one finger
can lift and carry himself,
and his floating energies

in the tranquil mass
of the bath half melt away
dreaming of angels
and deepsea weeds. Weight of flesh
almost imperceptible,

awash in its own
happiness; warmth of his blood
almost as warm as
the water's intimacies,
spreading through every vein.

The living body
can barely be distinguished
from the formless one
whose substance replaces it
with its every movement.

Someone is mingling
with the infinite fullness
surrounding him;
someone feels he is gently
dissolving. The whole body

is at present no
more than a pleasant dream
vaguely dreamt by thought.
The sweet moment mirrored with
limbs limpid in water's glass.

He observant of
and converser with himself
marvelling at all
the grandeur, the symmetry
of members he subjugates,

and the thinking head
is entertained by some foot
or other that comes
to the surface far away,
obeys as if by magic.

It beholds a toe
floating up, flexing itself,

a knee emerging
and sinking back into this
transparency, an island

extruded by waves
of some oceanic swell,
then by some caprice
plunged back again, down to
the very depths of the deep.

It is will itself
and the being's general
liberation that
find themselves recomposed in
the repose of the billow.

There lingers perhaps
in the close and steamy air
a scent whose flower is
complexity still
questioning the memory,

caresses, colours
naked being's vague desires.
Eyes lost, closing.
Contact with time dies away.
The mind opens veins of a dream.

James Kirkup *has sent us a translation into two* tanka *of a quotation from Valéry that appeared in* Télérama, *the French television magazine:*

Pas de doute, il faut s'appeler Valéry pour voir dans ces machins gélatineux des "*êtres d'une substance incomparable, translucide et sensible, chairs de verre follement instables, dômes de soie flottante, couronnes hyalines, longues lanières vives toutes courues d'ondes rapides, franges et fronces qu'elles plissent, déplissent*" etc. *(Christian Sorg, in* Télérama*).*

Jellyfish

Beings of matter
beyond compare, translucent
and sensitive, flesh

crystal, ridiculously
unstable, domes of drifting

silk, with hyaline
tiaras, long lianas
shivered all over
in racing ripples, fringes
and flounces of trailing shawls.

*[Neither James Kirkup nor the editors can trace the source of Sorg's quotation
though there are other jelly-fish floating through Valéry's work. Perhaps one
of our readers can enlighten us?]*

Paul Valéry

Translated by Claire Nicolas White

Paul Valéry *(1871-1945) was a friend and in his youth a disciple of Mallarmé, whose exalted view of poetry and the poet he shared. The 'Cantique des colonnes', first published in 1919 and collected in* Charmes *(1922), uses architecture as a symbol of poetic artifice, while the poem's shape on the page pictures the classical columns.*

Claire Nicolas White, *born in the Netherlands, is a poet, playwright, translator and art critic. Her most recent translations from the Dutch are Tim Krabbe's* The Vanishing *(Random House, 1993) and Adrian van Dis's* My Father's War *(The New Press, 1996). Her poems have appeared in many magazines, and she has taught creative writing at SUNY and elsewhere. She has lived in St James, Long Island, since 1947.*

The Canticle of the Columns

The gentle columns wear
their hats in the bright air
with lively birds for trim
that walk about the brim.

The gentle columns sing
a spindle-legged song
each silent voice suppressed
to mingle with the rest.

– What do you raise up high
so similar in face?
– To a perfect desire
we bring our studious grace.

With the weight of the skies
on our head we advance.
Oh voices truly wise!
We sing to please the eyes.

See how candid the tune!
What melody we draw
from the daylight at noon
created without flaw.

So chilly and golden
from our chambers we rose
awakened by the chisel,
lilies of pure repose.

From our crystalline beds
how rudely we were called!
And steely were the claws
that fit us to this mould

each one of us to groom
smooth as a fingernail,
to face up to the moon,
the sun, the Milky Way.

Handmaidens without knees,
smiling without a face,
a girl in front of these
feels her legs growing chaste.

Pious and similar,
our noses and our ears
tucked safely out of sight,
we are deaf to the weight

of temple on our brow.
Blinded eternally
we advance without gods
towards divinity.

Our ancient youthfulness
olive-skinned in the shade,
is proud of this perfection
born out of repetition.

A honey-coloured God
lies down to cover us,
daughters of golden section,
strong in our just proportion.

Content, in daytime he
sleeps on the table we
spread to him above
the altar to his love.

Incorruptible sisters
half chilly and half burned
we have taken for partners
leaves dancing in the wind

and centuries by tens,
civilisations past
a time so deep, it is
a measureless abyss.

With our similar loves
weighing more than the world,
we plummet through the days
like stones through the waves.

We advance into time
and our bodies divine
leave an essential trace
immortalised in rhyme.

Max Jacob

Translated by Christopher Pilling

Max Jacob *(1876-1944), friend of Apollinaire and Picasso, defies definition: he believed that personality was only 'a persistent error'. A Jew who converted to Catholicism late in life, he was arrested by the Nazis and died in Drancy.*

Translations by **Christopher Pilling** *and David Kennedy of prose poems from Jacob's* Le Cornet à Dés *(1917) appeared in MPT8. We include the French text of the poems here so that readers may appreciate their characteristic word-play, and the ingenuity of Pilling's versions. His translations of poems by Corbière appear in this issue.*

from **Les Œuvres Burlesques et Mystiques de Frère Matorel, Mort au Couvent de Barcelone** *(1912).*

For Children and Sophisticates

Through Paris of course
On your grey horse
Through Nevers don't lag
On your green nag
Through Issoire as pillion
On your black stallion
Ah! he's so fine and dandy!
Oh! so fine and dandy!
Tishoo!

The bell is tolling on
For my daughter Yvonne.
Who died in Castellane?
The general's wife, Roxane.
Who died in La Rochelle?
The colonel's niece, Belle!
Who died in Epinal?
The corporal's wife, Sal!
Tishoo!

And in Paris, darling Daddy,
What'll you give me, I'm not faddy?

I'll give you as a birthday treat
A hazel-nut hat, a neat
Satin vanity case
To hold in your hand to see your face.
A white parasol in silk, built
With acorns up the hilt.
A gilt-edged gown to use
As security and shiny orange shoes.
Only put them on
On Sunday, Yvonne,
A necklace and jewels
Tishoo!

The bell is tolling on
For my daughter Yvonne!
The Paris bell has tolled: it's said
It's time to go to bed
The Nogent bell is striking
And Daddy can't help liking
The idea of bed as well.
There goes the Going Gong, the Givet bell.

Oh no! not yet, Silly!
Buy me a Puffing Billy
You must! you must!
One that raises the dust
In front and behind.
Watch out, level-crossing ladies, mind!
Here comes Yvonne
Riding up on
Her iron horse, with daddy in tow
Hello! Hello!
Tishoo!

Pour les Enfants et Pour les Raffinés

À Paris
Sur un cheval gris
À Nevers
Sur un cheval vert
À Issoire
Sur un cheval noir
Ah! qu'il est beau! qu'il est beau!

Ah! qu'il est beau! qu'il est beau!
Tiou!

C'est la cloche qui sonne
Pour ma fille Yvonne.
Qui est mort à Perpignan?
C'est la femm' du commandant.
Qui est mort à La Rochelle?
C'est la nièce au colonel!
Qui est mort à Épinal?
C'est la femme du caporal!
Tiou!

Et à Paris, papa chéri.
Fais à Paris! qu'est-ce que tu me donnes à Paris?

Je te donne pour ta fête
Un chapeau noisette
Un petit sac en satin
Pour le tenir à la main.
Un parasol en soie blanche
Avec des glands sur le manche
Un habit doré sur tranche
Des souliers couleur orange.
Ne les mets que le dimanche
Un collier, des bijoux
Tiou!

C'est la cloche qui sonne
Pour ma fille Yvonne!
C'est la cloche de Paris
Il est temps d'aller au lit
C'est la cloche de Nogent
Papa va en faire autant.
C'est la cloche de Givet
Il est l'heure d'aller se coucher.

Ah! non! pas encore! dis!
Achète-moi aussi une voiture en fer
Qui lève la poussière
Par devant et par derrière,
Attention à vous! mesdames les garde-barrières
Voilà Yvonne et son p'tit père
Tiou!

based on **Avenue du Maine** from **Les Œuvres Burlesques et Mystiques de Frère Matorel, Mort au Couvent de Barcelone** *(1912).*

Off the Avenue du Maine

The managers can't manage
Unless they're managing menageries
On the Avenue du Maine.
The badger is
An animal whose adage
Is: I'm no man and not of an age
To manage managers or men
On the Avenue du Maine.
I live in badgeries
With budgies I engage
To man the set way home when
Menageries cause mayhem
On the Avenue du Maine.
But '*Budge*' is the word I use to them
Should they lack acumen.
It's all so undermining for badgers, man!
Mind! undermanagers all
Still manage *gadgies*
With pledges at the edges of credibility
Where managers stand to fall.
If undermanagers can't span
The archness of bridges
Between managers and men
Miners and minors might manage
To manoeuvre the undermined from their den
To deny ostriches on the rampage
And manic apemen in carriages
Without my vigilante budgies
Becoming twitchy hitmen
Of the Avenue du Maine
But since last-ditch kitsch is
Here to stay, many stand to freeze
Out on a bridge of civility
Badgering to budge menageries.

Avenue du Maine

Les manèges déménagent.
Manèges, ménageries, où?. . . et pour quels voyages?
Moi qui suis en ménage
Depuis . . . ah! il y a bel âge!
De vous goûter, manèges,
Je n'ai plus . . . que n'ai-je?. . .
L'âge.
Les manèges déménagent.
Ménager manager
De l'avenue du Maine
Qui ton ménage mène
Pour mener ton ménage!
Ménage ton ménage
Manège ton manège.
Manège ton ménage.
Mets des ménagements
Au déménagement.
Les manèges déménagent,
Ah! vers quels mirages?
Dites pour quels voyages
Les manèges déménagent.

The Rain

Mr Yousouf has forgotten his umbrella
Mr Yousouf has lost his umbrella
Mrs Yousouf, someone's stolen her umbrella
There was an ivory knob on her umbrella
What went into my eye was the tip of an umbrella
Didn't I leave my umbrella
Last night in the stand you have for any old umbrella?
I'll have to buy an umbrella
I never actually use an umbrella
I have a dust-coat with a hood to keep the rain from my *fontanella*
Mr Yousouf, you're in luck doing without an umbrella.

La Pluie

Monsieur Yousouf a oublié son parapluie
Monsieur Yousouf a perdu son parapluie

Madame Yousouf, on lui a volé son parapluie
Il y avait une pomme d'ivoire à son parapluie
Ce qui m'est entré dans l'œil c'est le bout d'un parapluie
Est-ce que je n'ai pas laissé mon parapluie
Hier soir dans votre porte-parapluie?
Il faudra que j'achète un parapluie
Moi je ne me sers jamais de parapluie
J'ai un cache-poussière avec un capuchon pour la pluie
Monsieur Yousouf vous avez de la veine de vous passer de parapluie.

During his blue period, Picasso did a comic strip of Max Jacob glorified, accepted into the French Academy, driven in a chariot to the Arc de Triomphe, wearing a toga and carrying an umbrella, and receiving a laurel crown from Pallas Athene in the Elysian Fields. Max, in the habit of saying his poems to Pablo, could well have penned 'La pluie' (from *Les Pénitents en Maillots Roses*, 1925) as a jest in response, as every line but one ends in *parapluie* and that one ends in *pluie* (rain). Or he may have written it as a horizontal umbrella poem in response to Apollinaire's almost vertical rain poem, 'Il pleut', (written in July 1914, published in *SIC* in 1916 and then in *Calligrammes* in 1918). Being bald, Max himself may have been quite content to do without an umbrella – he could have one in his imagination, and not just one, but a skyful à la Magritte. My '*my fontanella*' may be a far cry from the rain of the original, but the Italian word, rhyming with umbrella (a rhyme being absolutely essential here) means, as well as 'fontanelle' (a part of the body most likely to feel the rain when there's no umbrella), 'little fountain' – allowing me to be hand-in-glove with Max's childlike pleasure in word-games! Yousouf must be a Muslim mystic (souf = wool worn by ascetics) and mysticism was a Jacob trait. He read palms, cards and coffee grounds and saw, on a wall of his room where he had painted a landscape, a vision of God in yellow silk with blue facings.

Guillaume Apollinaire

Translated by Robert Chandler

Robert Chandler's *versions of poems by Guillevic and Paul de Roux appeared in* MPT *8, of Akhmatova and Tarkovsky in* MPT *10, of Sappho and Apollinaire in* MPT *13. The following text is adapted from the Introduction to his translation of a selection of Apollinaire's poems forthcoming in October 2000 from Everyman, who published his translations of Sappho. His translations of modern Russian prose (Vasily Grossman, Andrey Platonov) were published by Harvill.*

Robert Chandler writes: One of the first of Apollinaire's poems to make a lasting impression on me was 'Merveille de la Guerre'. This was unlike anything I had ever read before. Apollinaire's ecstatic description of the beauty of a night sky lit up by shell-fire and flares is entirely convincing, but deeply shocking to anyone who – like me at the time – unconsciously expects all war poetry to be like Wilfred Owen's. I now see this poem as a supreme example of Apollinaire's ability to give free rein to his imagination without ever losing touch with reality. I was shocked simply by the vividness with which Apollinaire registers a sad truth: that beauty and violence can live side by side. The battlefield did indeed have its moments of beauty and – as Norma Rinsler has pointed out in a fine article on Apollinaire's war poetry[1] – Apollinaire is not the only writer to have noticed this. Wyndham Lewis, for example, has written of the 'great romantic effects' of a night bombardment;[2] and the French writer Henri Ghéon described the night sky over the battlefield as 'the dance of night and the festival of speaking fire'.[3]

Apollinaire's war poems are still astonishingly unrecognized – even in France. And while many poems from *Alcools* – even quite slight ones – have been translated into English five or six times, most of the poems from *Calligrammes* have only been translated once, and few of the poems from the posthumous collections, *Poèmes à Lou* and *Poèmes à Madeleine*, seem ever to have been translated at all.

Chronologically, the war poems fall into three groups: those written while Apollinaire was undergoing training in Nîmes, those written while he served in the artillery, and – a smaller group – those written while he served in the infantry. The poems in the first group are for the main part exuberant; for all their naive optimism, they remain deeply touching. Apollinaire's excitement was shared by millions of people, and it is expressed vividly. Unlike most patriotic poetry of the time, Apollinaire's never dissolves into abstraction; poems such as 'At Nîmes' are full of precisely observed detail.

The second group were written while Apollinaire was serving in the artillery. (. . .) These poems are imbued with wonder, excitement and eroticism. They are not, however, escapist. In the first place, Apollinaire is entirely conscious of his wish to escape. One of his poems to Madeleine ends with the lines:

Are you a goddess like the goddesses the Greeks created so as to feel
      less anxious
I worship you O my exquisite goddess even if you live only in my
      imagination

Secondly, much of the imagery of even the most wildly erotic poems is derived from the war. It is as if Apollinaire would like to escape into sexual fantasy, but is prevented by the pressure of his day-to-day experience. The intensity of his desire to escape testifies to the depth of the horror he feels.

During his first six months of active service, Apollinaire was a gunner, positioned behind the front line and thus sheltered from the war's worst horrors. In November 1915 he was transferred, at his own request, to the infantry. After this transfer he wrote of 'the front line trench whose horror can't be described, let alone imagined'.[4] And in December 1915, in a letter to Madeleine, he wrote: 'Imagine to what extent one is deprived in trench life of everything that joins you to the universe. One is simply a breast offering itself to the enemy.' Life in the artillery now seemed like 'a country picnic, an excursion whose risks aren't much greater than those of mountaineering.'[5] The mood of the later poems in *Calligrammes* is correspondingly grimmer. There are still grimmer fragments that Apollinaire seems uncharacteristically to have censored, perhaps afraid that his readers would be uncomprehending. The following lines, for example, were not published during Apollinaire's lifetime:

Harden yourself old heart hear the piercing cries
Let out by the wounded in agony in the distance
Men lice of the earth O tenacious vermin

The free-verse poems in *Calligrammes* are remarkable for their imagery, for their visionary power. Many of the rhyming octosyllabics in *Alcools* are remarkable for the delicacy of their rhythms. It was only while translating this volume that I became aware of the power and depth of a group of poems where Apollinaire's musical, painterly and intellectual gifts are fused: the short lyrics in *Calligrammes*. These poems, however, are deceptively simple; I shall finish by discussing 'Exercise' in some detail.

Norma Rinsler has written with regard to the later war poems: ' The early optimism about a better future was gone. The only way to avoid fear was not to think of the future at all. (...) In *Exercice* (...) Apollinaire shows how this attitude detaches a man from life, so that the presence of death becomes less alien. His infantrymen, like Wyndham Lewis's, hardly notice the shells; like monks they have trained themselves to the patient rhythm of an ascetic life which expects nothing of this world, and thus is not afraid of leaving it.'[6] Wyndham Lewis also served in the artillery and Norma Rinsler is referring here to a passage from his autobiography: 'More German batteries were firing now, and a number of shells intercepted us. We met an infantry party coming up, about ten men, with earthen faces and heads bowed, their eyes turned inwards as it seemed, to shut out this too-familiar scene. As a shell came rushing down beside them, they did not notice it. There was no sidestepping death if this was where you *lived*. It was worth *our* while to prostrate ourselves, when death came over-near. We might escape, *in spite of* death. But *they* were its servants. Death would not tolerate that optimistic obeisance from them!'[7] The coincidence between this passage and Apollinaire's poem is remarkable.

Notes

1 'The War Poems of Apollinaire' in *French Studies*, April 1971, p169-186.

2 *Blasting and Bombardiering*, London, John Calder, 1982, p116 (cited in 'The War Poems of Apollinaire').

3 *Foi en la France*, Paris, 1916, p77 (cited in 'The War Poems of Apollinaire').

4 Apollinaire, *Lettres à sa Marraine 1915-18*, ed. Adéma, Paris, 1951, p58.

5 Rouveyre, *Apollinaire*, Paris, 1945, p241.

6 Rinsler, op cit, p177.

7 *Blasting and Bombardiering*, pp135-6.

The Cavalier's Goodbye

God! this soldiering's a delight
We sit around we joke and sing
The north wind and our sighs unite
I keep on polishing this ring*

God be with you! The trumpet call!
He trotted off across the rise
And there he died and left his girl
To laugh at fate in her surprise

* Here, and in 'For Madeleine alone', Apollinaire refers to the fact that soldiers used to make rings for their sweethearts out of fragments of aluminium from shells.

Flashes

The watch is beside the candle that burns quietly behind a
    screen made from the tin-plate of a jam tin
In your left hand you hold a stop watch which you will start
    at the right moment
With your right you are ready to centre the alidad of the sights
    triangle on the far-off flashes
You aim as you start the stopwatch and you stop the stopwatch
    when you hear the explosion
You note the time the number of reports the calibre the deflection the
    number of seconds elapsed between the flash and the detonation
You watch without turning away you watch through the gun-port
The rockets dance the bombs explode and the flashes flash
While all around can be heard the simple and crude symphony
    of the war
So my love in life we bring our heart and our attentive piety to bear
On the unknown and hostile flashes that adorn the horizon
    and people it and control us
And the poet observes this life and discovers the countless flashes of
    the mysteries that must be located
And known O Flashes O my dearest love

For Madeleine Alone

White moon you shine less than the hips
    Of my love
Dawns I admire you are less white
    Dawns I admire
Every day O hips so white
A hint of your whiteness
Lies deep in this aluminium
From which we make rings
In this zone where whiteness reigns
    O hips so white

Nothing Much

What a lot of them we've managed to kill
Fuck me
Strange it doesn't mean anything to me
Fuck me

A camembert for the Krauts
Fuck me Fire
A bar of chocolate for the Boches
Fuck me Fire
Each time you say Fire! The word changes into steel and then it
explodes over there
Fuck me
Take cover
Fuck me
Crack!
The buggers are answering back
Strange language isn't it Fuck me

Wonder of the War

How splendid these flares are that light up the night
They climb up onto their own peak and then lean over to
    have a good look
They're dancing ladies the looks they cast are their eyes
    arms and hearts

I recognized your smile and your vivacity

They're also the daily apotheosis of every one of my
    Berenices whose heads of hair have turned into comets
These gilded and glittering dancers belong to all times and all races
They give birth abruptly to children who have no time to do
    anything but die

How fine all these flares are
But it would be finer if there were still more flares
If there were millions of them their meaning complete and
    related like the letters of a book
All the same it's as fine as if life itself were to emerge from the dying

But it would be finer still if there were still more flares
Yet I see them as a beauty who flaunts herself then disappears
I seem to be at a great feast all lit up like the day
The earth is treating herself to a banquet
She is hungry and she opens her long pale mouths
The earth is hungry and she's feasting like Balthasar the cannibal

Who would have guessed we could go so far down the road of
      anthropophagy
Or that it could take so much fire to roast a human body
That's why the air has a slightly empyreumatic taste that really isn't
      unpleasant by God
But the feast would be finer still if the sky were feasting along with
      the earth
All the sky ever swallows is souls
Which is a way of not eating at all
And it's happy just to juggle with many-coloured lights

But I and all my company have flowed the length of the long
      communication trenches and into the sweetness of this war
A few cries of flame keep announcing my presence
I have hollowed out the bed I flow down branching
      into a thousand little streams that run everywhere
I am in the trench nearest the enemy and at the same time I
      am everywhere or rather I am beginning to be everywhere
I am beginning something that belongs to centuries to come
And that will take longer to make real than the fable of Icarus the airman

I bequeath to the future the story of Guillaume Apollinaire
Who was in the war and knew how to be everywhere
In the lucky towns in the rear
In all the rest of the universe
In those who die fighting their way through barbed wire
In women in cannon in horses
At the zenith the nadir the four points of the compass
And in the unique ardour of this eve of battle

And doubtless it would be finer still
If I could imagine that all of these things in which I am
      everywhere
Could enter me too
But in that respect there's nothing doing
For I may be everywhere now but inside me there's
      still only me

Exercise

Four bombardiers were on their way
To a small village in the rear
Layers of dust had turned them grey
They'd joined up earlier that year

They quietly talked of other years
And gazed at the vast plain ahead
A shell coughed near the bombardiers
Not one so much as turned his head

They only spoke of yesterday
Tomorrow seemed a waste of breath
They held to their ascetic way
This constant discipline of death

Guillaume Apollinaire

Translated by Cristina Viti

Cristina Viti is a translator, poet, storyteller and lyricist. Born in Milan, she has actively pursued the study of languages since childhood, both within and outside the education system, before and after moving to London. A selection of translation favourites and a collection of poems are forthcoming.

Mountebanks

On the plains a band of clowns
Skirt the gardens, walk on down
Past the graying inns they lurch
Across hamlets with no church

And the children, look, they're leading
The others follow on, they're dreaming
All the fruit trees bow and sway
As they wave from far away

They lift weights, square ones and round ones
They have gilded hoops, loud drums
Monkey and Bear so smart and so wise
Ask for pennies as they say their goodbyes.

The Gypsy

And the gypsy did know and did tell
of our lives held hostage by Night
when we said farewell it seemed right
that Hope should spring up from the well

Love heavy as a mad deprived bear
stood up to dance, our will was his tether
and the bluebird shook down one more feather
and the beggars forgot all their prayers

We know so well we will be damned

but we hope we'll find love on our way down to hell
that's why we muse as we walk hand in hand
on the future that gypsies foretell

The Betrothal

Spring lets her cheating sweethearts roam
Leaf-lazy they fall like feathers of blue
Shaken off the cypress that shelters the bird of blue

A madonna has gathered eglantines at dawn
Tomorrow she'll come for cloves hot and sweet
To line the nest of the doves she has sworn
To the pigeon, a night-time Paraclete

In the little lemon grove latecoming girls
Fell in love of the love we love tender
Their eyelids are faraway hamlets, little worlds
And among fragrant lemons their hearts are suspended

My friends have at last confessed their contempt
I drank the stars by the glassful
While I slept an angel exterminated
The lambs and shepherds of sad pastorals
False centurions brought vinegar
And tramps wounded by the purge were dancing
Stars of awakening, I knew none
The gas jets pissing blue flame in the moonlight
Undertakers tolling beermug bells
In the candlelight false collars fell
On great breakers of unkempt skirts
While masked babymakers from hell
Celebrated the births

It was an archipelago, this evening, our city
Women demanded love go down on bended knee
O river, river dark, it all comes back to me
The passing shadows weren't ever pretty

Oh I've lost all self-pity
And I cannot express my torment of silence
All the words I had to say have turned into stars
An Icarus flaps his wings to reach each of my eyes

I am the sun-carrier and I burn in the centre of two nebulae
What have I done to intelligence's theological beasts
The dead of yore
Have returned to adore
Me, and I
Who was hoping for the end of the world
Hear my own approaching instead, hissing
Like a hurricane

I had nerve enough to look back
The corpses of my spent days
Mark out the road I've taken and I mourn them
Some are rotting away in Italian churches
Or in little lemon groves that
Blossom and fruit
At the same time, any season
Other days have wept before going to meet their death in some bar
Where wheels of burning flowers turned
In the eyes of a half-breed who invented poetry
And roses electric still open
In my memory's garden

Oh forgive my ignorance
Forgive me for no longer knowing the ancient game of verse
I no longer know anything, I
Can only love
The flowers in my eyes turn back into flames, I meditate
Like the gods above
Benevolent towards the beings I haven't created
But if the time should come
When shadow finally solid
Multiplied giving tangible shape
To the thousand facets of my love
Oh then I would
See that it was good and rejoice.

I observe the Sunday rest
And praise idleness
How to, how to narrow down
This subtler and subtler science
Imposed by the senses
One is like mountains like the sky
Like cities, like my love, it resembles
The seasons, it lives

With the sun for its head and the moon for its severed neck
I want to feel endless ardour
Monster of my hearing you roar and weep
Your mane is thunder
And your claws echo the singing of birds
Monstrous touch has penetrated me it's
Poisoning me
My eyes swim away from me
And the intact stars are my peerless masters
The beast of all smokes has a blossoming head
And the prettiest monster
Tastes like the laurel and so must know distress

In the end I'm no longer scared of lies
The moon cooking like an egg on a dish
This necklace of raindrops will adorn the drowned girl
Here is my bunch of Passion flowers
Tenderly offered up by two crowns of thorns
Streets shine with long-ago rain
Diligent angels are working for me back home
Sadness and moon, they will wing it
All the blessed day
All the blessed day I've been walking and singing
A lady leaning at her window
Looked long at me as I walked away singing

On a streetcorner I saw sailors
Baring their throat to an accordion dance
I have given everything up to the sun, everything
Except my shadow

Sounding lines, bales, wails of sirens half-dead
Misty horizons swallow up the three-masts
Winds die away crowned with anemones
And sigh for the Virgin, pure sign of the third month

Templars on fire I'm burning amongst you
Grand Master, let us prophesy
I'm the sought-after fire pledged only to you
Your catherine wheel is spinning, oh beauteous beauteous night

Oh you who die young, I will blow out
The bondage-destroyer, the free flame of Ardour

My death will be glory and despair, I look out
As if I were sighting a target

Uncertainty, fake painted bird, you fell down
Sunlight and love danced back into town
And your gallant sons whether well- or ill-dressed
Built this great pyre, my courage's nest

Ever

                    Ever
Farther we'll go, never further
And planet to planet

Nebula to nebula
The don Juan of a thousand-three comets
Is looking for new stimuli
Even down here on earth
Oh he takes his ghosts
          seriously

And so many universes lost in oblivion
Tell me, who are the great amnesiacs
Who will be able to dissolve
The memory of this or that somewhere, where is
The Columbus we'll honour
For the forgetting of a continent
                              To lose

To really lose
So we can *find* again
                              To lose

Our life so we can
               win it.

Blaise Cendrars
Switzerland – French language

Translated by Cristina Viti

Blaise Cendrars *was born in Switzerland in 1887. After he ran away from home at the age of 16, his father sent him to St Petersburg, where he was employed by a travelling salesman called Rogovin, and witnessed the Revolution of 1905. In 1907 he moved to France, and became a bee-keeper, spending his spare time on the fringes of literary circles. An inveterate wanderer, and generally penniless, he travelled to Brussels, London (where he performed as a juggler in a music-hall), Russia, Antwerp, New York . . . This odyssey is reflected in his most famous poems. Cendrars joined the Foreign Legion on the outbreak of war in 1914, and was seriously wounded in 1915, losing an arm. After the war he travelled to South America and Africa, and worked in film with Abel Gance. His later writings are in prose, but a poetic prose that blends reality and dream. He died in 1961.*

Cristina Viti*'s versions of Apollinaire appear above.*

Easter in New York

> Flecte ramos, arbor alta, tensa laxa viscera
> Et rigor lentescat ille quem dedit nativitas
> Ut superni membra Regis miti tendas stipite . . .
> Fortunate, **Pange Lingua**

> Bend your branches, oh huge tree, relax but a
> little the tension of the viscera,
> And relent from your natural rigour,
> > Don't lacerate so cruelly
> > the limbs of the Supernal King.
> > Remy de Gourmont, **Le Latin Mystique**

Lord, it's an old book I open and read
on the day of your Name. Your Passion, your deed,

your anguish, your effort, your words so humane
weep down in the book like sweet gentle rain.

It is an old story a pious monk told.
He wrote of your death in letters of gold

In a missal he rested upon his knee
working slow, working steady, every day of the week.

Seated in his white robes, not once did he falter,
inspired by You, sheltered by the altar.

Time itself stood still in his doorway
as he forgot himself, intent on your portrait.

When the Vesper bells sang psalms in the tower,
the good friar thought it was beyond his power

to know whether his love, Yours, or the Father of mortals
was knocking so hard on the monastery portals.

I am like that good monk, tonight: a strange gloom
weighs on me, and some voiceless waif in the next room

waits behind the door, waits for my call.
It is You . . . It is God . . . It is me . . . or the Eternal.

I have never known You, not to this day,
as a child I have never knelt down to pray.

And yet thinking of You tonight I am scared,
my soul's your doleful mother as painted by Carrière.

Widow mother in black at the foot of your Cross
beyond all hope and tears, mourning, mourning such loss.

I know the Christs of all museums far and wide
But I feel You tonight walking right by my side.

I am bent and I'm feverish as I stride on down
carrying my shrunken heart into town.

Your split-open side blazes like a great sun
and your hands send sparks flying all round.

The windowpanes of houses are filled with blood
the women behind them are flowers of blood,

strange withered orchids, flowers shedding their spores
like upturned calyxes opened under your sores.

Your gathered blood, undrunk, they have let it slip past
they are lip-rouged, and they are lacy-assed.

The flowers of Passion are white like the tapers we carry,
they are the sweetest in the garden of Mary.

It was towards the ninth hour, Lord, at this time
that your sweet Head onto your Heart reclined.

I am sitting by the ocean shore
recalling German hymns of yore

describing in words so sweet, simple and pure
the beauty of your Face under torture.

In a church, at Siena, inside a cave,
on a wall, behind a drape, I've seen that Face.

And in a hermitage at Bourrié-Wladislasz
I've seen it in gold relief in a case.

It has two turbid cabochons for eyes
and peasants on their knees, they kiss your Eyes.

Veronica's shroud carries its print
and so Veronica is your special Saint.

It is the best of relics, displayed across the fields,
it heals the sick, exorcizes all fiends.

I'm pretty sure it's cured thousands that were deformed,
although I've never seen a miracle performed.

It might be, Lord, I lack goodness and faith
to see the splendour of your Beauty's rays.

And yet, Lord, I have braved a perilous voyage
to contemplate the cut beryl that holds your image.

Lord, I take my face into my hands and pray:
let this vicelike mask of anguish fall away.

Lord, my hands are on my mouth, please hear my prayer:
may I not lick the froth of ferocious despair.

I'm sad and I'm sick, perhaps because of You,
or perhaps of some other. Perhaps because of You.

Lord, the thousands you sacrificed for
throng daycare like lousy cattle – they're *the poor.*

From the horizons huge black ferry boats appear
and disgorge them pell-mell onto the pier.

Chileans and Kurds and Albanians,
Tibetans Sri Lankans Rumanians
they leap across the meridians like trained frogs
and they're thrown pieces of black meat, just like dogs.

This foul pittance, you know, makes their day.
Lord, have mercy on those with nowhere to stay.

Lord in the ghettoes the Jews still swarm like bees
not all come from Poland, but they're all refugees.

And I know that they put you on trial,
but give them a chance, Lord, they're not all so vile.

They're holed up under copper lamps in their shops,
Rembrandt loved to portray them wearing their frocks.

They sell weapons and books and old robes,
just tonight I have haggled over a microscope.

Oh! Lord, after Easter, there'll be no more You . . .
Lord, Have mercy on these shacks, and on the Jews.

Lord, the humble women who followed your calvary
are hiding away, polluted by men's misery.

They're slumped on rotting couches in their slums,
their bones dog-gnawed, and countless rums

conceal the vice that hardens in them like scale.
Lord, I try to talk to them, but my nerves fail.

I wish I were You so I could love prostitutes.
Lord, have mercy on prostitutes.

Lord, I am in the neighbourhood of good thieves,
of fences, ragamuffins, and must-leaves.

I think of the two thieves who were with you at the gallows,
I know you didn't disdain to smile down on their sorrows.

Lord, one would like a rope knotted into a noose,
but that don't come for free, son, the rope is twenty sous.

Now that old bandit knew how to philosophize
I offered him some opium to rush him to paradise.

And street musicians too, tonight, are on my mind,
the barrel-organ amputee and the fiddler who is blind,

the singer in her straw hat with paper roses;
theirs are the songs eternal, though not everyone knows this.

Lord, give them alms other than gas light flickering blue,
Lord, give them alms, big money down here too.

Lord, when you died the veil was torn and fell
what was behind, no one did ever tell.

The street's opening the night up like a gash,
full of gold, full of blood, full of fire and trash.

Those you whipped out of the temple as thieves
now flog passers-by with a fistful of misdeeds.

The Tabernacle Star, back then, took flight
and now burns on the wall in the crude showbiz light.

Lord, the Bank so brightly illuminated
is a safe where your death blood is coagulated.

The streets now deserted turn blacker.
I sway on the sidewalks like a drunken old slacker.

Scary darkness juts out from houses in big flaps,
hobbling steps approach with threatening taps.

I'm being followed. I daren't turn my head.
I'm scared. I'm fainting. I stop dead.

A hideous weirdo walks by and has me stagger
with a sharp look that cuts and hurts me like a dagger.

Lord, nothing's changed since the end of your Reign:
evil uses your Cross as its cane.

I trip down the dodgy steps of a café
the Chinese owners are like polished netsuké.

When they bend, their backs smile up at me
as I watch them while I drink a glass of tea.

It is a small teashop, lacquered red,
curious bamboo-framed chromos above my head.

Hokusai painted a mountain in a hundred ways.
I wonder how a Chinese would paint your Face? . . .

This image, Lord, of You, foreshortened,
brought a strange smile at first: I saw you martyred,

but your torment would have been portrayed
with more cruelty than Western painters displayed.

Your flesh would have been cut by the curved blades that swerve,
tweezers and combs would have scored your every nerve,

Lord, you'd have been pilloried without fail,
your teeth would've been pulled out, and then your nails,

huge black dragons would have hurled themselves at You
and blown your neck full of flames so red and blue,

your eyes and tongue would've been torn out, and that's not all,
Lord, you'd have been spiked on a long pole.

Thus you'd have suffered, Lord, the utmost shaming,
for there is no crueller torture than impaling.

And then they would have thrown you into a trough
for pigs and sows to come and gnaw your guts off.

Right now everyone's gone and I'm alone,
I'm lying on a bench against the wall.

I would have liked a church where I could kneel or sit down,
but there're no bells, Lord, in this town.

I think of tied-up bells: where are the sweet antiphonies?
Where are the ancient bells? Where are the litanies?

Where is the canticles' unadorned beauty?
Where the liturgies, music, long offices, duty?

Where are your nuns, Lord, and where are your fierce prelates?
Where is the white dawn, the Saints' immaculate amice?

The joy of paradise is drowned in dust,
the mystic fires don't burn, the stained-glass windows rust.

The dawn is slow in coming, and in narrow slum halls
crucified shadows are agonizing on the walls.

It's like a Golgotha in the night's faint glimmer
that we see, red on black, as mirrors shimmer.

Like a faded loincloth twisting around your waist
smoke curls under the lamp in lazy haste.

Right above, the pale lamp is hanging high
like your Head, sad, dead, bled white.

Weird reflexes are winking on the panes,
I'm scared – and I'm sad, Lord, to be sad and in pain.

Dic nobis, Maria, quid vidisti in via?
– The humble morning light, quivering.

Dic nobis, Maria, quid vidisti in via?
– Lost whitenesses like hands, shivering.

Dic nobis, Maria, quid vidisti in via?
– Spring's promise in my breast, thrilling.

Lord, the dawn has slipped in cold as a shroud
and has laid the skyscrapers bare in the clouds.

Already the city is alive with sound,
trains thunder and roll underground.

The trains bound and rumble and shudder away,
bridges are seized by the railway.

The city trembles. Cries, smoke and fire
and the raucous wail of steam sirens.

Fevered from gold sweats this throng
jostle and cram down tunnels dim and long.

In the maze of plumed roofs the sun's so murky,
it's your Face gobs of spit have made dirty.

Lord, I return tired and mournful, alone . . .
my room is bare as a tomb . . .

Lord, I'm all alone, I've a fever . . .
my bed is cold as a coffin . . .

Lord, I close my eyes, my teeth are chattering . . .
I'm too alone. I'm cold. I'm calling . . .

A hundred thousand spinning tops dance before my eyes . . .
no . . . a hundred thousand women . . . no . . . a hundred thousand
      cellos . . .

I think, Lord, of the hard times . . .
I think, Lord, of the gone times . . .

I no longer think of You. I no longer think of You.

New York, April 1912

from **Dix-neuf Poèmes élastiques**

F.I.A.T.

Split eardrums

I envy your rest, o factories
anchored like great liners on the edge of town

If only I were as empty
as you are after your parturitions
but these tyres are vexing my back and I have
little red lightbulbs at the end of each nerve

Your beautiful white chamber so functional, metallic
the cradle
the rare noises of
Sainte Clothilde hospital, I am
always fevered
Paris Addresses

O to be in your place
beautiful hairpin bend!
For the first time I envy a woman
I want to be woman
In the universe
In life, to be
and to open oneself to the childlike future
I who am dazed instead
and Blériot-blearied
I get into gear, see?

My pen is cantering,

so beat it!

April 1914

My Dance

The poet like a wandering Jew
like a metaphysical don Juan
is denied citizenship in Platonic republics

Friends and relations . . .
You've no customs left and no habits as yet
Better escape the tyranny of reviews
Literature
Bare life, misplaced pride
Mask
And Woman, the dance proposed by Nietzsche
who wanted to be teacher
Woman . . .
But what of irony?

Continuous come-and-go
Special roaming
All men, all countries
You know, that's how you're no longer a charge:
you just
disappear . . .

I am this genteel type crossing ever*un*changing Europes in fabulous
    express trains and looking out of the window in dismay
You see I am no longer interested in the landscape
but the landscape's *dance,* ah well, the *dancescape,*
Paritatitata
I guess it still
gives me a spinning thrill

February 1914

Blaise Cendrars

Translated by Martin Bennett

Martin Bennett's *translations of poems by Primo Levi, Pasolini, Pavese, Quasimodo and Ungaretti appeared in MPT 15.*

Fetishes

I
Muscles of mahogany
Two embryonic arms
A stomach that's gone AWOL
Manhood at attention

II
Who've you got it in for
You who go about
Fists on haunches
Worryingly off-centre
Not quite as stout
As you might wish?

III
Knot of wood
Acorn-shaped head
Hard and refractory
A godling blank of face
Blank of sex
Cynically hilarious

IV
Envy has gnawed away your chin
Covetousness kept you erect
And thin
What you lack by way of a face
You make up for in geometries
Even trees could not better
Teenage icon from the Planet X

V

A man and a woman
Equally hard-featured equally nude
He less plump but just as strong
With hands on his tummy
That money-box mouth

VIII

I wanted to flee the chief's umpteen wives
The stone of the sun has shattered my head
There in the sand
Nothing remains but my mouth
Wide open and conserving moisture
Like something for which a fit of Englishness
Strictly forbids translation

IX

Bald as a ball-bearing
He has only a mouth
This member dangling about his knees
Two truncated feet

[British Museum, London, February 1916]

from **Nineteen Elastic Poems**

1 Journal

Christ
It's more than a year now that I've not thought of You
Since I wrote Easter my last poem but one
My life has changed since then
Yet I remain much the same
There on the wall are the paintings I've done
They open up strange views into myself and bring my mind back to You

Christ
Life
That's what I've dug up

My paintings make me ill
I'm over-passionate
The whole world's turned orange

I've spent a sad day thinking of friends
And reading the paper
Christ
Life crucified in the daily broadsheet I hold open with outstretched
    arms
Wingspans
Flares
Ferment
Cries
One would think an aeroplane's crashing
It's me

Passion
Fire
Cheap paperback
Newspaper
It's no use trying not to talk about oneself
Every so often a scream is the only option

I am the other
Too touchy by half

4

I. Portrait

He sleeps
He is awake
All at once, he's painting
He paints a church and he paints with a church
He paints a cow and he paints with a cow
With a sardine
With heads, hands, knives
He paints with a bull's dismembered member
He paints with the squelching passions of a little Jewish village
With Russia's vast countryside and all its pent-up sexuality
For France
Matter-of-factly
He paints with his thighs
He has eyes in his backside
And suddenly it's your portrait
You the reader
It's me
It's him

It's his fiancée
It's your neighbourhood grocer
The cowherd
The midwife
There are tubs full of blood
Where the new-born are washed
Delirious skies
Mouths of modernity
The Eiffel Tower turned corkscrew
Hands
The Christ
The Christ it is him
He spent his childhood on the Cross
Every day he commits suicide
Suddenly he's no longer painting
He was wide awake
Now he's asleep
He strangles himself with his tie
Chagall's astonished to find himself still living

II. Attic
Stairs, doors, stairs
Then you're there
Covered with visiting cards
His door opens like a newspaper
Swings shut
Not unpleasurably you catch your breath
Chaos, lovely chaos
Aesthetics stretched to its limits
Photos of Leger, a painted wooden parrot
Works in progress or aborted
Empty bottles of every size and shape
We guarantee the absolutely purity of our tomato ketchup
States a label
For a window there's a calendar
And o the high drama once snappy cranes of lightning not so far
    overhead start unloading the sky's barges and skips
The rain falls in torrents
You could be out at sea, a thousand leagues adrift
Yet inside it's warm, even somewhat stuffy

Russian cossacks
Dusty icons
Suns like meat going rotten

Sleepwalkers Goats
Winter and insanity
Djinni or smoked fish or broken-down shoes
Suddenly the lamp and everything else turning double
Quadrupling
The thousand and one empty bottles
Morose delectation
Chagall
Chagall
His ladders of light

7 Hamac

Face like a donkey's
Gare Saint-Lazare's complicated clock
Apollinaire
Advances, dawdles, stops
Nomad of Europe
And the west
Why aren't you accompanying me to America?
At the quayside I broke down and wept
New York

Our ship shakes the crockery
Rome Prague London Paris Nice
Books heaped like a breakwater
Oxo-Liebig paints his cabin-walls

Blunderbusses versus coconuts
Julie ou j'ai perdu ma rose

Futurist

A long time you wrote in a painting's shadow
Your dreams wove Arabesques
You more blessed than any of us
Since Rousseau completed your portrait
With stars
Those bardic carnations which the English call *Sweet Williams*

Apollinaire
1900-1911
For twelve years France's only poet

9 Sputterings

Over the wireless
Rainbowish dissonances
Noon
Midnight
All corners of the universe trading pet expletives

Sparks
Fibre-optic dictionaries
We're in contact
Clouds like liners
North south east and west
Now near now distant
As bells sound across time-zones
Time becomes a numbered whirr
Paris-Midi announces a German professor has been devoured
  by cannibals in the Congo
I drink a toast
The Economist offers poetry-postcards at a price of minus ten Euros
  per dozen
A pretty pass when astrologers think they can juggle constellations
No wonder nothing's clear
I interrogate the heavens
The Weather Centre announces mist and fog
No futurism
No simultaneity
I'm out of here
Like a message in a bottle
I leave this poem for whom it might concern
And for whoever it might not

10 Stop Press

OKLAHOMA, 20th January 1914
Three convicts have got hold of revolvers
They kill their jailer then seize the prison keys
Next they've broken out from their cells
The death toll rises as they shoot four of the guards in the yard
Meanwhile they've taken the girl-stenographer hostage
Outside the gate a carriage is waiting
Other guards empty their guns in the fugitives' direction
As they drive off at top speed

Some guards leap on horseback and gallop in pursuit
A shooting match breaks out
The girl-stenographer is wounded by a stray bullet

Another bullet kills the horse that's pulling the coach
The guards can now approach
They find the convicts' bodies riddled with bullet-holes

Mr Thomas, former member of Congress and a prison-visitor,
Offers the girl-stenographer his congratulations

Poem-telegram, stop press from *Paris-Midi*

11 Bombay-Express

The things that I've seen
Have cured me of any notions of suicide
Everything's jumping
O high-heels and rollerskates
Music under my finger-nails
Taxis straining outside station doors

I never liked Andy Warhol
Reserve a particular aversion for Jeff Koons
Enough of art and artists
Ballyhoo and bridges
Pistons and trombones
The more light that enters my head
The less I pretend to know or comprehend
Only that your caress
Sets my heart fluttering like an atlas

This year or the next
Art-criticism is as silly as Esperanto
Le Havre or Brindisi or Folkestone
Goodbye goodbye

There are whims as muscular as pole-vaulters

Let me carry you away
You whose laughter turns the whole world vermilion

18 The Head

The guillotine is the masterpiece of the plastic arts
Its click
Unleashes perpetual movement
Everyone's more or less subconscious of Christopher Columbus's egg
How he managed to stand it upright
Against all odds, one end squashed flat
An egg stable and unwobbling, worthy of an inventor
Archipenko's sculpture goes one better
Egg with its ovoid still intact
Maintained in intense equilibrium
Like an immobile top
Upon its animated tip
The speed of it
Shedding iridescent waves
Zones of colour
As it spins within the deeps
Naked.
New.
Complete.

Blaise Cendrars

Translated by Alan Passes

Alan Passes, *born in 1943, was raised in Switzerland, France and Britain. He has published a novel,* Big Step, *short stories and poems, and had a number of his plays produced. He is currently writing and directing an experimental piece for radio, commissioned by the Arts Council. Ten years ago he began to study anthropology, and was awarded a doctorate for his work on an Amerindian people (the pa'ikwené) who live in Brazil / French Guiana. He is co-editor of* The Anthropology of Love and Anger: the aesthetics of conviviality in Native Amazonia, *forthcoming in 2000 from Routledge. We publish here extracts from his translation of Cendrars's long poem, which was written a year later than 'Easter in New York'.*

Prose of the Trans-Siberian Railway and of Petite Jehanne de France

– dedicated to musicians

At that time I was in my adolescence
I was barely sixteen years old and had already forgotten my childhood
I was sixteen thousand leagues from my birth
I was in Moscow, in the city of the thousand and three belltowers
    and the seven stations
And the seven stations and the thousand and three belltowers did
    not suffice me
For my adolescence was then so ardent and wild
That my heart blazed in turn like the temple of Ephesus or the
    Red Square in Moscow
As the sun sets.
And my eyes lit up ancient paths.
And I was already such a bad poet
That I did not know how to go to the very end.

The Kremlin was like an immense Tartar cake
Encrusted with gold, with the giant almonds of the white cathedrals
And the honeyed gold of the bells . . .
An old monk read to me the legend of Novgorod
I was thirsty
And I deciphered the cuneiform characters
Then, suddenly, the pigeons of the Holy Ghost flew up in the square
And my hands flew away also, with the sound of an albatross

And these, these are the last reminiscences of the last day
Of the last journey of all
And of the sea.

. . . .

At that time I was in my adolescence
I was barely sixteen years old and had already forgotten my birth
I was in Moscow and wanted to feed myself with flames
And could not get my fill of the belltowers and the stations
         which constellated my eyes
Cannon thundered in Siberia, it was war
Hunger cold plague cholera
And the silted waters of the Amur swept along thousands of carcasses
In all the stations I saw the last trains pulling out
No one could leave for tickets were no longer being issued
And the departing soldiers would much rather have stayed . . .
An old monk sang the legend of Novgorod.

I, the bad poet who wished to go nowhere, I could go everywhere . . .

. . . .

Tears well up deep in my heart
If I think, Love, of my mistress;
She is but a child that I found thus
Pale, unsullied, in the depths of a brothel.

She is but a child, fair-haired, cheerful and sad,
She does not smile and never cries;
But in the depths of her eyes, when there she lets you sip,
Trembles a silver lily, the poet's flower.
She is soft and silent, and without reproach,
And quivers slowly at your approach;
But when I go to her, this way, that way, gaily,
She takes a step, then shuts her eyes – and takes another.
For she is my love, and other women
Have but dresses of gold over great flaming bodies,
My poor friend is so alone
She is naked, and has no body – she is too poor.

She is but a guileless, slender flower,
The poet's flower, a poor silver lily,
So cold, so alone, and already so faded
That tears come to my eyes if I think of her heart.

And this night is like a hundred thousand others when a train speeds
through the night
– Comets fall –
And a man and a woman, however young, delight in making love.

. . . .

"Blaise, tell me, are we so very far from Montmartre?"
We are far, Jehanne, you've been travelling for seven days
You are far from Montmartre, from the Butte which fed you from
          the Sacré Coeur against which you used to huddle
Paris has disappeared and of its huge blaze
Only eternal ashes remain
The falling rain
The swelling peat
Siberia swirling
The heavy rising sheets of snow
And the little bell of madness shivering like a dying wish in the blue sky
The train throbs in the heart of leaden horizons
And your sorrow giggles nervously . . .

. . . .

I would like
I would like never to have gone on my journeys
Tonight a great love torments me
And despite myself I think of little Jehanne de France
On an evening of sadness I have written this poem in her honour

Jeanne
The little prostitute
I am sad I am sad
I will go to the *Lapin agile* to recall my lost youth
And drink a few small glasses
Then I will head back home on my own

Paris

City of the lone Tower of the great Gibbet and the Wheel

   [Paris, 1913]

Jean Cassou

Translated by J Kiang

Jean Cassou *(1897-1986) was born in Bilbao but spent his adult life in Paris, where he directed the Museum of Modern Art for twenty years. He was an anti-Fascist in the Spanish Civil War and a leader of the French Resistance in the Second World War. As well as poetry, his writings include novels, short stories, biographies of painters, historical studies, translations from Spanish and journalism. His* Thirty-three Sonnets Composed in Secret *were written while he was imprisoned during the Occupation.*

Jacqueline Kiang *was born in New York and lives in Paris. She is an engraver and watercolourist, and received the Guy Levis Mano Prize for poetry illustration in 1984. Three of her translations of Cassou's sonnets appeared in* MPT 1.

The Thirty-three Sonnets *were published clandestinely by Editions de Minuit in 1944, with an introduction by Aragon. Eight of the sonnets, together with part of Aragon's introduction, were translated by Timothy Ades and appeared in* MPT 9.

IV

I dreamed that I carried you in my arms
from the courtyard to your darkened room.
You seemed a sister to cherished creatures
whom I adore, but I did not know you.

It was a moonlit night with hoarfrost,
a vibrant night, echoing with adventure.
And as I tried to discover your face,
I felt you light and trembling with cold.

Then I lost you, like so many other things,
the pearl of secrets, the saffron of roses,
offered to my heart in dreams or reality.

With every sun so painfully reshaped,
memory's ciphers, enigmas all lead me
to a paragon of sorrow, keen and lucid.

X

Rose of Alexandria . . . It was a song
spangled and streaked by rockets on the beach.
And the night effervesced all over, as it does
when the first celebration takes place at home.

Yes, a childlike joy rushed us onto the balcony
and we gazed down at the dancing in the village.
And yet, beloved, your face was shadowed,
and our hands trembled as we turned that page!

Then, with summer, hope came too and brusquely
caught us in its clutches, fantastic hope!
There it was! – Perhaps it is still with us.

We sense something prowling alongside our lives,
across the forest where our steps become wearier,
a ferocious beast, never appeased.

XI

My companion, you will only have known the dark
side of my star and its sightless eyes,
unyielding mouth and its aridity,
only the austere aspect of a mortal shadow.

Who else should have had my glances and the tuneful
liquid cupped in my hands when it was light?
My exotic promises soon slipped away
to the distant rim of the fatal sphere.

Return to your own light and your own strength,
– your angel still prospers – and be
a Narcissus without pride, desire or tears,

bewildered and blushing to know yourself lovely.
You alone have let me offer at my altars
a felicity fashioned from alarms.

XII

Hand in hand assiduous dreams pass in turn,
turning all my trodden paths into one dark lane,
blowing such a devastating sigh over it
because in your heart, where my story is known,

I can only reflect illusions and grief
and languishing stars on a meandering road,
a conjuncture of dissonant chords that trail
without echo or measure or mirrored semblance.

If I drink at your sky it is because
my bitter cup has filled it to the brim.
My eyes are dazzled when my grieving perceives yours,

gaping holes of flame multiply all around,
as many blue ocelli as in the peacock's tail,
your glances ripped on the rocks of my night.

XIV

Like the secret sense of a child's roundelay,
hasn't everyone longed to hear his own voice one day
and see his own gaze and the marks
of his footprints as his steps move away?

My poorly beloved, Time, that arrant impostor
robbed us of our time and wily, flew away,
leaving us a shred of his spiteful song
as a lullaby. It sometimes seemed to me

that this life was not entirely our own.
But don't you see, it was surely she and no one else.
The wandering girl with wasted hands, who came to sit

in the cold chimney corner one windy evening,
just look at her, look at her fearful glance
of a forlorn bird, of a languishing star.

XV

When we enter that Chinese city,
I shall limp a little but I shall know love.
Poor pawns, crouched at ploughs or else
at feverish walls and gates and towers

will rush to guide us to the cisterns,
and a mild moon, sister to the day's end,
will welcome us with a retinue of lanterns
and a battery of cymbals and muffled shouts.

I shall go clinging to the folds of your beloved gown
and to the furtive kisses that your eyes give,
eyes of paradise, of music and prayer.

Oh! What an unexpected recompense
to discover, like twin glints of stars lost
then lit again, the breath of our buoyant souls.

Tahar Bekri
Tunisia

Translated by Patrick Williamson

Tahar Bekri, *son of a station manager, attended Franco-Arab schools and studied French literature at the University of Tunis. In 1964 he began writing poetry in both French and Arabic. A militant in the student movement opposed to Bourguiba's single-party régime, he was arrested and imprisoned in 1972 and again in 1975. In 1976 he left Tunisia and went to Paris, where he was awarded a doctorate in French-language Mahgrebin literature in 1981. His first collection,* Le Laboureur de Soleil *(The Ploughman of the Sun), was published in 1983, followed by collections in both French and Arabic. He currently divides his time between writing, teaching and research; he became a lecturer at the University of Paris X-Nanterre in 1995.*

Patrick Williamson, *born in 1960, graduated in European Studies and has taught English at professional training schools in Paris, where he now lives. The most recent volume of his own poems is* Lobster Eating *(Macan Press, 1997), and he has translated many French and French-Canadian poets. His versions of poems by the Vietnamese poet Cu Huy Can appeared in* MPT 9.

from **Le Laboureur de Soleil**

The Lines are Trees

The lines
are trees which grow
with the heart of the earth
in their roots

The lines
are springs which flow
with the mountain's offering
in their memory

The lines
are leaves which blow away
with the racing wind
in their veins

The lines
are forests which walk
with the thunderstorm's song
in their throat

from **Fleuve Oued Pays Mêlé**

Segura, Murcia

How many rivers must you bear
in days being born
beyond the bridges that remember
beyond the shivering mornings
the silences of laurel trees surprised by your footsteps
here and there like letters stolen from the night
in the seditious high walls

There you are again river an untiring confidant
the fir tree consoles you not as you flow
in sprightly memory
nor does the sea embrace your old memories
carried away by the unfaithful source
leaving the noria of your bared heart there
hanging above the seguias of the ephemeral

Oued, Gabès

Tell me if the eucalyptus hardens
your bark if the stone still
listens to the wind if the sand keeps
our dwelling places in a burning memory
The waiting for waters mingles absence
and the return of mirages On the gullied banks
the years dry up like miserly fig trees

A friend of floodwaters weary of monotonous banks
tied in knots in the bed of bitter laurel trees
you shout to ungrateful valleys at the top of your voice
I carry your echoes away songs braving the thunderstorm
fire wedding in the wild skies
this palm grove born of my entrails
standing between my eyes and the sea

Two Francophone poems

Translated by MA de Brito

Mark Angelo de Brito *was born in London in 1963, and studied at the Guildhall School of Music. He has published one book of original verse,* Bigistong *(Darengo: London 1996), a poetic history of the West Indies. The present translations of Haitian and Cuban poetry belong to an anthology (in progress) entitled* Limbs of Osiris, *which brings together material from several languages by both continental and diasporic Africans. Mark de Brito is co-editor of the journal* Seshat: cross-cultural perspectives in poetry and philosophy. *Current projects include an extended poem under the title 'Heron's canoe'.*

René Depestre (1926-)
Haiti

Text: *Journal d'un animal marin: Choix de poèmes 1956-1990*. Gallimard: Paris 1990 (Extract from *Un arc-en-ciel pour l'occident chrétien*. Présence Africaine: Paris 1967)

Atibon-Legba

Je suis Atibon-Legba
Mon chapeau vient de la Guinée
De même que ma canne de bambou
De même que ma vieille douleur
De même que mes vieux os
Je suis le patron des portiers
Et des garçons d'ascenseur
Je suis Legba-Bois Legba-Cayes
Je suis Legba-Signangnon
Et ses sept frères Kataroulo
Je suis Legba-Kataroulo
Ce soir je plante mon reposoir
Le grand médicinier de mon âme
Dans la terre de l'homme blanc
A la croisée de ses chemins
Je baise trois fois sa porte
Je baise trois fois ses yeux!
Je suis Alegba-Papa

Le dieu de vos portes
Ce soir c'est moi
Le maître de vos layons
Et de vos carrefours de blancs
Moi le protecteur des fourmis
Et des plantes de votre maison
Je suis le chef des barrières
De l'esprit et du corps humains!
J'arrive couvert de poussière
Je suis le grand Ancêtre noir
Je vois j'entends ce qui se passe
Sur les sentiers et les routes
Vos cours et vos jardins de blancs
N'ont guère de secrets pour moi
J'arrive tout cassé de mes voyages
Et je lance mon grand âge
Sur les pistes où rampent
Vos trahisons de blancs!

O vous juge d'Alabama
Je ne vois dans vos mains
Ni cruche d'eau ni bougie noire
Je ne vois pas mon vêvé tracé
Sur le plancher de la maison
Où est la bonne farine blanche
Où sont mes points cardinaux
Mes vieux os arrivent chez vous
O juge et ils ne voient pas
De bagui où poser leurs chagrins
Ils voient des coqs blancs
Ils voient des poules blanches
Juge où sont nos épices
Où est le sel et le piment
Où est l'huile d'arachide
Où est le maïs grillé
Où sont nos étoiles de rhum
Où sont mon rada et mon mahi
Où est mon yanvalou?
Au diable vos plats insipides
Au diable le vin blanc
Au diable la pomme et la poire
Au diable tous vos mensonges
Je veux pour ma faim des ignames
Des malangas et des giraumonts

Des bananes et des patates douces
Au diable vos valses et vos tangos
La vieille faim de mes jambes
Réclame un crabignan-legba
La vieille soif de mes os
Réclame des pas virils d'homme!

Je suis Papa-Legba
Je suis Legba-Clairondé
Je suis Legba-Sé
Je suis Alegba-Si
Je sors de leur fourreau
Mes sept frères Kataroulo
Je change aussi en épée
Ma pipe de terre cuite
Je change aussi en épée
Ma canne de bambou
Je change aussi en épée
Mon grand chapeau de Guinée
Je change aussi en épée
Mon tronc de médicinier
Je change aussi en épée
Mon sang que tu as versé!

O juge voici une épée
Pour chaque porte de la maison
Une épée pour chaque tête
Voici les douze apôtres de ma foi
Mes douze épées Kataroulo
Les douze Legbas de mes os
Et pas un ne trahira mon sang
Il n'y a pas de Judas dans mon corps
Juge il y a un seul vieil homme
Qui veille sur le chemin des hommes
Il y a un seul vieux coq-bataille
O juge qui lance dans vos allées
Les grandes ailes rouges de sa vérité!

Atibon-Legba

I am Atibon-Legba.
My hat comes from Africa,
just as my bamboo cane,

just as my ancient grief,
just as my old bones.
I am the patron saint
of door-keepers and lift-boys.
I am Legba-Bois, Legba-Cayes.
I am Legba-Signangnon
and his seven Kataroulo brothers.
I am Legba-Kataroulo.
Tonight I plant my reposoir,
the great medicine-tree of my soul,
in the White man's land,
at the crossing of his ways.
I kiss his door three times;
I kiss his eyes three times.
I am Alegba-Papa,
the god of your doors.
Tonight it is I,
the master of your trails
and of your White man's crossroads,
I the protector of the ants
and plants of your house.
I am chief of the gates
of the human mind and body.
I come covered in dust.
I am the great Black ancestor.
I see, I hear what goes on
on paths and roadways.
Your White man's hearts and gardens
hold hardly any secrets from me.
I come all worn out from my travels,
and I hurl my great age
on the floors where your White man's
betrayals crawl.

O you Alabama judge,
I see in your hands neither pitcher
of water nor black candle.
I do not see my vèvè drawn
on the floor of the house.
Where is the good white flour?
Where are my cardinal points?
My ancient bones arrive at your home,
O judge, and they see no bagui
in which to deposit their sorrows.

They see white cocks.
They see white hens.
Judge, where are our spices?
Where is the salt and the hot pepper?
Where is the ground-nut oil?
Where is the roasted corn?
Where are our stars of rum?
Where are my rada and my mahi?
Where is my yanvalou?
To hell with your tasteless dishes.
To hell with white wine.
To hell with apple and pear.
To hell with all your lies.
I want yams for my hunger,
malangas and pumpkins,
bananas and sweet potatoes.
To hell with your waltzes and tangos.
The ancient hunger of my legs
calls for a crabignan-Legba.
The ancient thirst of my bones
calls for robust, manly steps.

I am Papa-Legba.
I am Legba-Clairondé.
I am Legba-Sé.
I am Alegba-Si.
I draw from their scabbard
my seven Kataroulo brothers,
and I change my terracotta pipe
into a sword,
and I change my bamboo cane
into a sword,
and I change my large African hat
into a sword,
and I change the trunk
of my medicine-tree into a sword,
and I change my blood
you have spilt into a sword.

O judge, here is a sword
for each door of the house,
a sword for each head.
Here are the twelve apostles of my faith,
my twelve Kataroulo swords,

the twelve Legbas of my bones,
and not one will betray my blood.
There is no Judas in my body.
Judge, there is a single old man
who watches over the way of men.
There is a single old fighting-cock,
O judge, who hurls into your path
the great red wings of his truth.

Note

The title 'Atibon-Legba' is the name of a *lwa* or divinity of Haitian *vodoû*, a religion
which derives in large part from the Fon of Benin. The Fon in turn are historically
indebted to the Yoruba: the name 'Legba' originates from the Yoruba 'Elegbara'.
This poem belongs to a dramatic sequence in which a White American judge and
his family are confronted by an epiphany of *lwa*. Names with hyphens which
include the element 'Legba' are aspects of the same divinity. In *vodoû*, each
principal divinity has a family of manifestations which sometimes function as
separate entities. The Kataroulo brothers are aspects of Legba-Kataroulo. The
reposoir is a tree which serves as a shrine for a *lwa*. Each *lwa* has his or her favourite
tree: the *reposoir* of Legba is the 'medicine-tree' (*tatropha cureas*). A *vèvè* is a ritual
diagram, usually drawn with flour on the ground, which represents (and
summons) a *lwa*; the *bagui* is the sanctuary of a *vodoû* temple. *Rada* and *mahi* are
rites – the names derive from African place-names; the *yanvalou* and *crabignan-
Legba* are ritual dances.

Léopold Sédar Senghor (1906-)
Senegal

The following poem is translated from Senghor's French version of a Bantu (blacksmith's?) invocation to fire. One can only speculate how much of the poem is 'traditional' and how much Senghor.

Fire which men watch in the night, in deep night,
Fire, you who burn and do not yourself get hot, who glow and
    are not burnt,
Fire, you who fly without body, without heart, who know neither
    hut nor hearth,
Clear fire of palm leaves, one without fear invokes you.

Enchanters' fire, where's your father? Where's your mother?
    Who reared you?
You are your father. You are your mother. You pass and leave
    no print.
Dry wood does not beget you. You do not have ash for offspring.
    You die and do not.
The wandering soul is transformed into you, and no one knows.

Enchanters' fire, spirit of the netherworld waters, spirit of the
    upper air,
You radiance who glow, firefly who cast light on the swamp,
Bird without wings, substance without body,
Spirit of the power of fire,
Hear my voice: one without fear invokes you.

Pem Sluijter
The Netherlands

Translated by Shirley Kaufman

Pem Sluijter *has worked as a journalist and for the Ministry of Foreign Affairs in The Hague, and has edited a quarterly on Third World problems. Her first collection of poetry,* Roos is een en bloem (Rose is a Flower), *was published by De Arbeiderspers in 1997; it was awarded the C Buddingh Prize for the best first poetry book in the Netherlands.*

    Shirley Kaufman, *who has published seven volumes of her own poems, and translations from Hebrew and from Dutch (she contributed to both our Dutch/Flemish issue, No.12, and our Palestinian/Israeli issue, No.14), has received the Shelley Memorial Award for lifetime achievement from the Poetry Society of America. She is co-editor of* The Defiant Muse (Loki Books), *the Poetry Book Society's Recommended Translation for Spring 2000, reviewed in this issue. The poems here have been translated with the author.*

Moerheim 1944

Crawling from under the rhubarb leaf
to the edge of the pond,
vegetable garden with the bustle
of weeding and snails dropping
behind me – I was far from the house.

My house on the canal
where the billeted enemy
wore boots – but I was more afraid
of the colour of frogs the colour
of lily pad and the small toad that
flashed over feet in a brown suit:
their throbbing throats and mine.

Beyond grew roses and Russians
were on their knees weeding the strawberry bed.
They might have shared
the secret of the child's tight-fisted hand,
the torn piece of a silk
parachute. If you saw a friend
not an enemy walk in the neighbourhood,
then you carefully
unfolded two fingers.

Jewish Poet

After her blue days
dressed like King David –
I saw her walk with a black
feather duster. Did she
follow the path of the angels
who left Satan
behind
in the streets of Berlin?

I can still see her
now as she stood then
in black
on the Mount of Olives
with her feather duster. Sweeping
each day, she says: God is dead,
or in any case far away.

New Year

The coveted terebinth
has lost its leaves:
all appearance wilts
as light follows darkness
the thinnest red
chases after the sun –
behind it new days
of fratricide smoulder.
I look out on the failure of gardens
I've chosen, myself a garden
that no longer gives water.

What does it mean
seven women
clutching one man?
Help me
explain this –
when you toss riddles at me
not being
watered I
come up
with nothing.

Violence masses above us
like the mountain exalted
above the hills: no people has ever
beaten swords into ploughshares

yet in Manila Cory prays
for rebels who give roses and in Accra
behind the crumbling slaveforts
(one named *longsuffering*) a car
proclaims: Let us not hate Whites.

Thirsty Land

Thirsty land this.
Slope after slope
it shakes itself like a dog.
Without drinking. Nothing.
The stony face
uplifted.

This land.
It doesn't want to rise up or
lie down.
Not ever bending,
terribly still,
speaks only for itself.

Nachoem Wijnberg
The Netherlands

Translated by Alissa Leigh

Nachoem M Wijnberg, *one of the best young poets in the Netherlands, has published seven books of poems and two novels, the second of which,* De joden *(The Jews) appeared in November 1999.*

Alissa Leigh *is a translator from Russian and Dutch, and is presently working for the Institute of War Documentation / Yad Vashem in Amsterdam.*

Tasks

A man walks into a café,
asks for coffee, puts so much sugar in it that the cup overflows,
drinks the coffee, asks the woman behind the bar for a light
for a cigarette he has already put in his mouth, gets a light, pays.
Early in the morning a man walks into a restaurant
which is being cleaned and asks the first person who looks at him
for a warm meal and a place where he can sit and rest.
Something happens to a man like the death of an only child,
something that makes his life different than he had imagined it thus
      far,
and he tells people about it who didn't intend to get to know him.
A man is left in a forest with two kinds of tree
and at the bottom of some hills there are treeless spaces
with slides and swings and merry-go-rounds which he has to power
      himself.
A man is put in possession of a story about his life
until the moment something bad happens to him and it is
left up to him whether he uses it or not.

It's still yours, even if I take it back

I remember a time I ran out on the beach.
I ran to and fro and in the sand there were only my own
footsteps.
I kept running; I didn't get tired.

A good table, far from Siberia.

I am very good at appropriating other people's

memories, in order to find later they had always been,
as the one undressed says to his undresser
it was already yours.

I open a bottle of champagne, a better bottle than before,
and apologise again.

My arm is gripped by another with fear
For his memories.
What am I to do with a stranger's memories
without which he can't go on?

What are those beautiful memories to him now;
they're not worth anything anymore!
                                        He says,
if he could, he would put them out with the garbage.

This concludes with the entrance of them dressed up as memories,
bowing to the left and right.
                                    A farewell performance
and all it raised is for them only.

Come see, aren't they sweet?

I've drunk champagne all my life.
The glasshandarms intertwined so that I couldn't tell
from which glass.

With what intention?
To make what retrieval more difficult?

                        An old photograph
of a busy street where I too walked at that time,
look to see if I'm in it,

whether my face doesn't happen to look at me. Look,
that was me, that you now know for certain what happened to me
            afterwards
makes you look a long time at this photograph.

Use time to stand in a line

and look back through the line
as if the eye openings stay in the same place

and the bodies can be turned and stretched
until all the openings coincide,

but there is no convincing beginning like a convincing ending,
like: but I spoke to him yesterday.

Look, like a photograph, and my face
isn't in it any more.

I bought a box of chocolates,
the first thing I bought in a store,

and I paid for it with coins I had picked up from the street.
On my way home I dropped the box
and those to whom I gave it didn't mention about the broken chocolates.

I wanted shoes I had seen.
Those who gave me money first thought they were too expensive.
When I got on the bus home I forgot the box
and when I came back to the bus stop it was gone.

I got money for new ones right away.

I got a present.
It was exactly what I wanted.
Everything I might tell
and for which I might be asked I would tell.

If I had more of them I could open
a gift shop
and if I knew someone who would wait in the store all day
for a customer like me

while outside light and warmth make sick children scream
with pain,

dry the grass in the gardens but throwing water
over them now would parch it.

Another present I forget to give myself,
it's not even that I had decided I should be able to do without.

How does the skin feel today,
like amazing nakedness?

We know each other so that it doesn't matter.

You didn't have to ask,
it was already yours.

Epitaph

Smiling he rode
into the middle of the battlefield
and even his horse was smiling

through the freezing air
he swung the point of his sword
in a circle soundlessly

naming his name
adds nothing to his honour

The Idols

The beggars held
the city in their power
they sat
on the cathedral steps

No one could pray
without losing all his money

they forced the sculptors
to use their bodies
as models
for new bodies of the Christ
and to fasten them to the crosses

the beggars sat
straddle-legged on the cathedral steps
while they let themselves be sketched

they slept there at night
between burning candles
rolled in carpets
so that no one could pray in secret

Tarjei Vesaas

Norway

Translated by Roger Greenwald

Tarjei Vesaas *(1897-1970), eldest son of a farming family in Telemark, became one of the giants of Norwegian and Scandinavian fiction. He won the Venice Prize in 1952 for a volume of stories, and the Nordic Council Prize in 1963 for the novel* Is-Slottet *(The Ice Palace). His work has been widely translated; eight novels have been published in English. Five volumes of his poetry were published in his lifetime and a sixth posthumously in 1970.*

Roger Greenwald *grew up in New York and lives in Toronto. He has earned major awards for his poems, including the CBC Radio /* Saturday Night *Literary Award (1994), and has published a book of poems,* Connecting Flight *(1993), several award-winning volumes of poetry in translation from Norwegian and Swedish, and two novels translated from Swedish. The poems here are taken from his forthcoming book,* Through Naked Branches: Selected Poems of Tarjei Vesaas *(Princeton University Press, 2000).*

The Footprints

On the secluded beach
there's no one now.
The mountains above are scorched.

An arc of sand, bitterly abandoned,
covered by one person's tracks! abandoned,
deserted after a harrowing wait.

The mountains above are scorched.
Someone has been here
and paced and paced
– but no one came across *this* lake.

The sand was completely closed off by strange mountains.
The yellow sand
with its last, lonely tracks.

Hurried footprints, caved in.
Just countless depressions in the sand.
The trail of your young foot in a frenzy,
your soft steps, in thirst, before you fled.

Your best dream, for no one.
Your golden form, wasted.
Splendid powers, for no one, no one
– while the black cliffs looked on
with streaks down their features
from previous lives.

The Boats on the Sand

The boats on the sand have drawn together
as if in a council of elders.
They stick their snouts together
and are silent and understand
(most things),
as old boats do.

O, how long their bodies are.
Low and sleek on a beach.
Their wood is darkening
and they are quietly decaying.
Made for water,
and to be destroyed by water.
Even now they're three-quarters in it.
What they don't know about the wet
no one knows.

They haven't settled anything
at their council.
All day they've lain there, motionless.
Boats in the home port they love.
Four of them on a stretch of sand.

Per Wästberg
Sweden

Translated by Harry D Watson

Per Wästberg, *born in Stockholm in 1933, is well-known as a critic and columnist as well as for his work with PEN and Amnesty International. He has published novels and essays, and several books of poems.*

Harry D Watson *is the editor of the Older Scottish Dictionary at the University of Edinburgh. His version of Wästberg's sequence, 'On Death', appeared in MPT 11.*

from Three-liners (Life Fragments)

*

A change in the weather sets the snow ablaze
On a slope where sand-martins gather.
I lick your lips, seal our love from the inside.

Clambered out of my unwieldy zip-suit,
Settled down on you, heavily, like a depression.
Suddenly found myself unimaginably loved.

*

Just because I was wrong about the unicorn,
Ignatius Loyola and penis-envy,
You surely needn't doubt my love for you.

The sheets, still creased from your fragrances
Hang between apple-trees. The goldfinch lets fall his flute
Between our bodies.

Love turned up like a late summer guest. Hard to grasp that others
Entered your body, and the world, before me. There is nothing of you
That I discovered myself.

Before, I also rang when you weren't at home.
Now I sleep on your side when you're away.
That way we lose less time with each other.

*

There's an erotic vocabulary I've long since used up.
When I knead your shoulder my wrist brushes against your nipple.
We manage most things without words.

Our glances so shameless they stayed embedded in each other.
My soul said: "You can't carry on like this."
The body replied: "Let's discuss that later."

I run to you as one runs towards traffic lights
In the distance: wondering if I'll make it
Before they change.

*

I remember suddenly how excited I was
The first time I folded up your dress and laid it
Over my shirt on the chair.

*

During the night our backs rub together like rowing-boats
At the same mooring-ring. The timbers showing signs of wear, the years
Holding them tight. We are floating.

*

One begins by loving someone for what's familiar,
But gradually one also begins to love
What one doesn't understand.

*

Your eyes darken, a flock of jackdaws swerves through them,
You don't see me. But on the banisters our hands
Meet unexpectedly, just like in one of my love-stories.

*

You sleep, breathing hard in staccato unrest. I don't wake you, I'm
At the mercy of your dreams. You've taken off your wedding-ring.
The skin's lighter there. Your hand, unprotected.

*

You spread your fingers as if there was nothing left
To grip. I taste your absence, moistly intimate
But unknown. Like tongue-tip to tongue-tip in the dark.

*

Driving home alone at high speed through a night
As full of holes as a worn umbrella
I feel your hand come between my hand and the wheel.

*

Feelings and states can die out like animal species.
My innocence left me without my noticing it.
Rubbed the rust from the knife-blade. Brought out the shine of love.

Review

by Richard Smith

Alain Bosquet, *Stances perdues – Lost Quatrains*
Translated from the French by Roger Little
Poetry Europe Series No. 6.   Dublin: The Dedalus Press, 1999.

"Lost" could mean, sadly, things that were left too long. A note tells us that before he died in 1998 Bosquet had retained forty-one self-reflective quatrains out of about two hundred that he had collected from the margins of his other manuscripts. It may be that he failed to find the best way of relating them to each other, that for him there were still details to improve. The text itself refers to his sense of defeat, as he felt time running out, and the very attempt to make a choice of marginalia may reflect a certain helplessness. There is also one fragment of a poetic autobiography, in the form of an imaginary questionnaire that he answers with the flippancy such formalities may, in real life, deserve. In the context of the works he published, the interest of this one is, then, marginal. Yet in it Bosquet both affirms and illustrates his qualities. In the questionnaire, for example, he suggests that his besetting sin, or chronic illness, is *la luxure du verbe*. The quatrains illustrate what this meant. They are the product of his incessant quest for innocent-looking but double-edged formulations, for the finality of a rhyme, balanced by the open-endedness of a surprise. The surprise stems often from his addiction to words and things. He strives for concision, and there is also effusiveness in the naming of sundry objects, plants, animals, in his Chekhovian appetite for life. His best friends, he says, are the sort of things you find in the toolshed: boxes with nails in, watering-cans, jam-jars, keys; at the same time, what pleasure to name a toucan! An internationalist, one of those writers who have chosen the French language, whilst helping to make frontiers irrelevant, he deserves the many translators who have responded to his appeal, amongst whom, where English is concerned, Roger Little stands out, along with Beckett. Little is surely the one, if willing, to take on the task of editing an English version of the collected poems, *Je ne suis pas un poète d'eau douce*.

In the present instance, Little does show a few signs of haste. He provides only one rhyme, sometimes just an assonance, per quatrain, where Bosquet has two – but this usually works in English. There are moments, however, when we need to consult the original: "set off trembling with anxiety" is not as clear as "*partir, l'angoisse au coeur, à l'aventure*". And though the poet may score goals that the translator misses, there appear to be some that Little aims at, even if Bosquet did not. A hint of "luxation" (dislocation) in "la luxure du verbe" is an example. Little renders this as "a dislocated lust for words", though any dislocation is an effect, not a characteristic, of the lust. At this point in his text, the concluding questionnaire, Bosquet fills in entries as an interrogator might fill in an official form, "for the record", in the third person. Little does not appear to see this. Under "*Sports?*" for example, he translates the entry as "I play . . .", whereas "Plays at being nobody" might give the right tone. This could help with the claim the poet makes under "*Patrimoine?*", a question which helps Bosquet to consider the cultural baggage, given his forbears, that he brought with him. To this question, the answer is a paradox: "an equator of his own invention", or, as Little has it, "of its own invention". Bosquet refers, surely, to an aspiration he had, and which was indeed part of his heritage, to "invent" what his life taught him was already in place, a base-line for a world order giving idiosyncrasy and autonomy their due. In that task, Little is his ally. The quatrains are nearly always both faithful renderings and new poems that speak, surely, to readers who have no French. A single page provides a sample:

After the body's betrayal, the soul remains:
constricted breath resembling a kiss.
Exist or die, enjoying praise or blame?
I am a centipede: come tread on this.

*

Shout it out loud: I'd style in every pore,
words in my soul and writing everywhere,
in my blood and lungs. So what if death
discharges flabby forms of corruption here!

Review Article

by Richard Dove

Hans Magnus Enzensberger, *Selected Poems*,
translated by HM Enzensberger and
Michael Hamburger
Newcastle upon Tyne: Bloodaxe Books, 1994

Hans Magnus Enzensberger, *Kiosk*
translated by Michael Hamburger with
additional translations by HM Enzensberger
Newcastle upon Tyne: Bloodaxe Books, 1997

The Doctrine of Agility: On HM Enzensberger's English Poems

There is something faintly ridiculous about endeavouring to review
Enzensberger. It is not just that his more than 40-year career has an
exemplary trajectory; nor that so many critics have already had their say;
but that his work is too diverse – each project a new departure – to admit
of generalisation. One is also uncomfortably aware that the author
himself has always mistrusted interpretation: his 1955 investigation into
that key proto-modernist Clemens Brentano repeatedly accentuates
'mystery' and 'inexhaustibility'; and in the introduction to the *Museum
of Modern Poetry* (1960), a consciously postmodern attempt to taxonomise
what he felt to be the already distant modernist phase (1910-45), we
come up against a warning against all 'isms', an insistence on the
inherent obscurity of all poetic utterance, and the following stern verdict:
'The poem always proves right vis-à-vis its interpreters.' All the same,
there are currently two reasons why one should not evade the challenge
of coming to some sort of terms with Enzensberger's *oeuvre*: the author
celebrated his 70th birthday some seven weeks before the end of the last
century, and a genuinely representative selection of his poems is at last
available in English.

I

There can be little doubt that Enzensberger is best known for his political
work, both in poetic and essay form. As he has acknowledged, this was
biologically inevitable, a product of the 'awareness of catastrophe'
which comes of being 15 in 1945. Such an awareness dictates his resolve
to remember the dismembered past (one of his most haunting poems,
dedicated to Nelly Sachs, is called *Those who have vanished*), and to seek

– surrounded by what he perceived to be a conspiracy of silence – to prevent 'the Final Solution of tomorrow'.[1] It also explains why he continues to believe in the 'necessity' (pragmatically lower-case rather than blindly Hegelian) of the 'political awakening' which made the FRG 'inhabitable' in the Sixties (*Die Zeit*, 20.1.1995). Enzensberger has repeatedly advocated the necessity of change, of 'getting history moving', as he put it in a 1969 interview with a Cuban magazine.[2] What he does not mention is how necessary he himself has been for Germany: his first collection came out in the year (1957) in which Adenauer won an election with the slogan 'No experiments', and his work – in both thematic and formal terms – has been one long refusal to accept such negative authority.

On the level of lifestyle, he was arguably the first 'cool' German: titles like *Call it love* (1957), or the way he systematically threw in such irreverent interpolations as 'warum nicht' ('why not') and 'meinetwegen' ('for all I care') to wrongfoot readers with Prussian monocles, helped to define an alternative republic. On the level of political awareness, he was Germany's only discernible 'angry young man', or rather the only poet who still seemed to be cognizant of Juvenal's dictum *Si natura negat, facit indignatio versum*. Even though he emerged with a whole panoply of voices, it was undoubtedly the satiric decibels which made the Fifties turn in their centrally-heated grave: 'here let us build tabernacles,/on this Aryan dump of scrap [. . .] this is the frozen-up waste,/this is successful madness, this dances/in needy mink, on broken knees,/in amnesia's eternal springtime'(*Language of the Country*). Typically, it is not from some remote romantic perspective that Enzensberger attacked the all-too-free market economics of the time. His philippics presuppose intimate knowledge of the economic base: 'Where a profit margin away from the poor rich the rich poor/smash their cinema seats for sheer joy' an early tirade runs, and the way he forcibly yokes together 'Qui la sua voce soave', 'Zu Befehl' and 'LIBOR' in a 1991 poem shows that he has never tired of unravelling the complicated dialectic of capitalism. Even Pound's (or rather Bunting's) famous false etymology DICHTEN = CONDENSARE is mercilessly dragged down into the marketplace in *Telegram Counter 12.12 am*: 'messenger paid, all that's valid here is/the hard poetics of binding charges:/condensare! On the soiled wall/*Keep it brief* Death, squandered heart,/*Keep it brief*, use plain text please:/*mi dulce amor*'(1957).

So what is Enzensberger's exact political position? This is a question which has exercised people, not only in Germany, for decades. He has certainly employed Marxist techniques of analysis, but his eminently practical streak precludes any millenarian illusions: 'Shortly before the millenium dawns,/they're boiling nappies'(*On the Problems of Reeducation*). Not least through his editorship of *Kursbuch* (1965-), he was effectively the godfather of the student revolution, the obvious exponent of Willy Brandt's imperative 'Dare more democracy', but the 1965-66 altercation with Peter Weiß demonstates that, for Enzensberger, 'positions' are provocative makeshifts to be abandoned when they have served their purpose or proved to be wrong-headed. Experience, etymologically related to experiment, is the biggest abstraction he is prepared to countenance, and there are abundant signs that he has little time for theories, whether Platonic or poststructuralist.[3] Maybe this is because he has such a sharp eye for contradictions, less in a Marxist than in a strictly ocular sense: '[. . .] if you are walking in a demonstration through Neukölln, for example, and someone calls out 'A socialist West Berlin!', as people did in those days, and you see the women up at the windows looking down, leaning on cushions and not believing their ears, then – if you've not lost all your marbles – you will have an *arrière-pensée*, in other words it will dawn on you that there must be a further thought behind the thought being expressed by the demonstration. There is, after all, an *arrière-pensée* behind every thought, and it is often the more interesting of the two'(*Die Zeit*, 20.1.1995).

Over and above his commitment to the progress of democracy in Germany and further afield, it is this unerring sense of detail which makes Enzensberger's political poems distinctive. *In the Old Days*, a 1980 text which gives short shrift to the nostalgic expectations set up by the title, contains the highly concrete confession: 'In the age of fascism/I'd no idea I was/living in the age of fascism./The place was teeming with piano-teachers.' A more monumental instance is *Karl Heinrich Marx*, whose purpose is intimated by the inclusion of the unfamiliar second given name: five compulsively symmetrical stanzas bring out the facticity underlying a legend. Enzensberger works with the evidence of brown daguerrotypes and fading letters to reconstruct the shabby dialect of matter, including a dejected excerpt from a letter to Engels of February 1866 on *Das Kapital* ('economic shit'), which lies behind the dialectical materialism. At a time (1964) when Marxism elicited blind faith in many quarters, Enzensberger's sarcastically sympathetic study flies in the face of political correctness by relying exclusively on the evidence of the eyes: the pillars holding up this poem are the six applications of 'I see . . .'[4] The last stanza reads:

[. . .] Gigantic zaddik
I see you betrayed
by your disciples:
only your enemies
remained what they were:
I see your face
on the last picture

of April eighty-two:
an iron mask:
the iron mask of freedom

The moribund Marx as a kind of philosophical descendant of the Man in the Iron Mask? One is free to deploy rhetorical terms, starting with paradox or oxymoron, to try to come to grips with that final image; but its jagged complexity refuses to be glossed over, and can stick in the memory for a quarter of a century or more like a distorted question mark.

Another reason why Enzensberger's political texts have the impact they do may be connected with the fact that a consistent standpoint is impossible to identify. At times one fancies one hears the well-starched tones of the political scientist: 'There's only a difference of degree/ between murderers and victims' (*Didactic Poem on Murder*). At others one stumbles across a cynic pointing a cosmopolitan lamp at the murk: 'False consciousness, say the philosophers./If only that was all that was wrong [. . .]'(*What is false*). But often there is a kind of spin which seems to owe most to Jarry's pataphysics or to Dada: 'Even our sighs/went on credit cards'(*Short History of the Bourgeoisie*). Or maybe even to Monty Python, as in the following dig at the Leviathan State, written at a time when Old Labour was in office in the UK: 'Man's struggle against man,/ according to reliable sources/close to the Home Office,/will be nationalised in due course,/down to the last bloodstain./Kind regards from Thomas Hobbes'(*Cold Comfort*). The austere, Dantesque *Purgatorio* (1964) is made more disquieting by the surreal changes rung on the disembodied refrain: 'Will [st.1 Herr Albert Schweitzer; st.2 Herr Adolf Eichmann; st.3 Monsieur Godot]/ please go to Transit Information'. Genre specialists can debate whether this is in fact surreal, grotesque, or whatever, but the effect is not lost on the *lecteur moyen sensuel* because of its very resistance to pigeon-holing; it is an instance of 'the resistance of the specific and concrete' which Enzensberger values.[5] The point is that one never knows where one is with this author: as in the case of an underground fighter, 'personal style' of the kind which turns the 'property' of a writer's early work into the 'symbol' of his later work[6] is a liability, and surprise the ultimate weapon. One rhetorical device which he uses like a hand-grenade on a whole host of occasions is the asyndeton, as in the last three lines of the third stanza of *Old Revolution* (1991), a poem in which Cuba functions as an allegory of the process first diagnosed in the 1974 essay *On the Ageing of the Revolution*:

[. . .] A sleepwalker in front of ten microphones
is preaching to his tired island:
After me nothing will follow.

It is finished.
The machine-guns glisten with oil.
The shirts are sticky with cane-juice.
The prostate has had it. [. . .]

One of Enzensberger's most uncanny talents is his ability to catch the spirit of a particular historical moment in a handful of lines or a single image. An example which springs to mind is *Memory* (the German title *Andenken* appears to allude to Hölderlin's elevated late meditation on love and heroic deeds): 'Well, as far as the 70s go,/I can be brief./ 'Enquiries' was engaged the whole time./The feeding of the five thousand/took place in the Düsseldorf region only.' Another example from the same collection, *At Thirty-Three*, the psychogram of a disillusioned Trotskyist, may well come to be the last word on the depressed Seventies: 'When she weeps she looks like nineteen'(1980). He crystallises the post-prandial melancholy of the Economic Miracle in a single barbarously objectless sentence in *Middle Class Blues:* 'We have nothing to conceal./We have nothing to miss./We have nothing to say./ We have.' And the gist of Glucksmann's polemic *Les maîtres penseurs* seems to be foreshadowed in nineteen scarily infantile words uttered by a chorus of Philosophy Department members in *The Sinking of the Titanic*: 'Hegel is smiling,/filled with *schadenfreude*. We daub his face/with an inky moustache. He now looks like Stalin'*(Dept. of Philosophy)*.

There is no way either that the *homo politicus* retreats into the background in the later work (one reviewer resorted to a slick play on prefixes in 1989 – '*aufgeklärt*'/'*abgeklärt*' –to insinuate that Enzensberger had abandoned the *via activa* in favour of the *via contemplativa*). If he writes that the headache of the subject in *The Employee* (1980) is 'unpolitical', the context makes it clear that this is far from approbation. And the opening section of the most recent collection, *Kiosk*, bristles with politics. *Privileged Instructions*, for instance, appears – *inter alia* – to be responding to the right-wing attacks on asylum-seekers' hostels in the early Nineties: 'It is forbidden to set fire to persons./It is forbidden to set fire to persons in possession of a valid residence permit [. . .]'. Although every two steps forward entail at least one lurch backwards, progress is not something Enzensberger ever appears to be indifferent about for long. His shot-up metaphors betray as much: '. . . in the bomb craters of progress'*(The Frogs of Bikini)*. If one did require an abstract statement of his political position, one would probably have to be content with the following dialectical, not to say Heraclitean utterance: 'Short-term hopes are futile, long-term resignation is suicidal'*(Kursbuch* 11, 1968,169).

What other aspects are there to his achievement? For one thing, he is a kind of phenomenologist of what – in a 1988 essay – he calls the 'average exoticism' of contemporary life. A random example is *Asphodels*

(1995), which casually reflects ('Funny . . .') about a gnostic on the fourth floor who is still awake, knocking incessantly on a heating pipe in an unidentified tenement block in an unidentified city where it is beginning to snow, where no shoe-laces are to be had, and where the machine-gun fire in the banking district has subsided; then comes an outlandish peripetia which reveals a perspective only superficially reminiscent of WC Williams: 'But in the fridge there are / a couple of asphodels, / just in case.' In this mood or mode, Enzensberger (like Lautréamont before him) seems exclusively interested in the adventitious conjunction of *disiecta membra*, but the title quietly insists that there is an intenser, symbolic charge: asphodels, it dawns on one at some point, are flowers that bloom eternally in the fields of the dead (cf *Odyssey* XI, 538ff). There is more involvement than meets the eye in other of Enzensberger's anatomies too: whether of the infantile suicides circling the wet square on their howling Hondas in some unnamed German neighbourhood (*Residual Light*); the ecstasies in the no-stopping zone in Munich (*Leopoldstraße*); the new dawn, rosy-fingered because of the agonistic interplay of gases, in Berlin just after the wall came down ('Throngs of pilgrims / in the pedestrian precinct, / searching for identity / and tropical fruit'; *The New Dawn*); or indeed of the 'Nirvanas at prices to suit every pocket' (*Some Advantages of Civilisation*). This is because the speaker's characteristic distance is essentially strategic: 'I talk about what is to be said, what is a 'burning issue', as though it were any old thing which didn't concern me.'[7] It is a strategy which can make his poems sound Martian *avant la lettre*: the man who wrote 'and they build you boxes / in which you drive, live, die' in 1991, described lichen in the following terms nearly thirty years before: 'It is the earth's / slowest telegram, / a telegram that never arrives' (*Lichenology*). And it certainly allows him to look dispassionately through the eyes of such heterogeneous things as the chattering classes with their sanctimonious bad faith (*Song for those who Know*), the 'ancient owls of the earth' (*The End of the Owls*), and the apparatus in a bathroom staring coldly at twentieth-century anthropos: 'Suicide too / doesn't cause the porcelain / to frown' (*Bathroom*). Whether he is drawing on the *Simultanstil* of the Expressionists or the synoptic style of the later Benn, it is patently one of Enzensberger's aims to provide an unflustered and – as it were – classical chronicle of the eminently unclassical *Reizüberflutung* ('deluge of stimuli') of modern life:

The reasons for the massacre must be looked for in the 13th century. That's what I read this morning at breakfast.

That bees are not deaf but hear with their antennae, was made known in Stanford, California.

Neckties are now worn again a little wider;
this was proved to me by a junk mail missive from 33102 Paderborn.

Time is not a parameter but an operator,
my friend the philosopher confided to me.

Information learnt on a single Tuesday [. . .]

Which is not to say that the sudden sharp swerve in the middle of this
particular poem *(An Encounter of the Other Kind)* does not bring us out
onto a very different road – the information in question is recited to the
neighbour's cat, and two alien metaphysics 'graze' one another while
they share a kipper. Such 'unmotivated' swerves are typical of a writer
who has never been a friend of consistency, at least not for its own sake,
as his 1981 essay *Goodbye to Single-Mindedness* makes plain. Readers are
advised to fasten their seat-belts before setting out on a ride in one of
these verbal machines.

So far, the emphasis has fallen on Enzensberger's role as a critical
analyst and annalist. But if he is a satirist, he is also (in George Steiner's
phrase) a friend. His Demosthenesian anger often obscures the fact that
he is unsparing of praise where praise is warranted, even though
panegyrics such as St John Perse's *Eloges* and Rilke's *Sonette an Orpheus*
have been a rarity in the 20th century.[8] This is not merely a formal feat:
although it might make academic sense to argue that the 'friendly
poems' which open his début collection (experiments with pastoral
styles in the tradition of Theocritus, Huchel, Eich, and others) are merely
an idyllic foil for the 'sad' and 'angry' sections that follow, there is an
incontestably warm – which is not to say uncool – tone in a great many
of this poet's texts. Not least when he is speaking up for unsung
phenomena, such as the 'mysterious/and commonplace' comb which
adorns a commonplace, mysterious woman *(The Comb)*:

[. . .] Blazing tortoiseshell. True enough, it too
lacks a few teeth. Oh, admire –
anyone can say that. – Forgive me,
I mean only that which nobody needs,
that about you which makes no impression at all [. . .]

Or stupidity, 'you the often maligned, who in your slyness/often
pretend to be stupider than you are, protector of all the frail,//only to
the elect do you grant the rarest of your gifts,/the blessed simplicity of
the simple'*(Ode to Stupidity)*. Or survivors, like the hare incarcerated in
a deserted data-processing centre in a 1991 poem ('Soft coward,/ fifty
million years/ older than we are!'), which hobbles past man 'into a

future/rich in enemies/but nourishing and rank/like dandelion'(*A Hare in the Data Processing Centre*). It may be typical of Enzensberger's complexity that he should filter an almost Leibnizian vision of a future of unlimited opportunities through the large eyes of a hare, but it is also typical that he should look beyond man's self-inflicted nihilism and detect something which seems to vindicate Celan's legacy: 'there are/still songs to be sung on the other side/of mankind.'[9] Like his main translator Michael Hamburger, Enzensberger is himself a survivor. And ultimately it is perhaps in such biographical terms that one must read his guarded refusal to give up on experience: 'There are bits of landscape left/if you look for them . . .'(*Residual Light*). Or his defence of the syllable '*schön*': 'trampled underfoot in the evening,/beauty rises bright and early,/new and sturdy, a fearless witness'(*Why I say 'schön'*). Or his declaration that lyric poetry is as indestructible – if superfluous – as weeds growing by the wayside (*FAZ*, 14.3.1989). Indeed, the close of the poem *Old Couples* (1991) sounds almost like a programme: 'There is much to be seen/when the lights go out'. Enzensberger knows more than many writers about darkness, but one senses that he finds something hopelessly inappropriate – whether incongruous or downright ungrateful – about grand abstractions like *le Néant*. It is a rather less valetudinarian descendant of Chamfort who declares: 'As long as someone has not cancelled his standing orders at the bank, he shouldn't talk to me about Resignation'(*Die Zeit*, 20.1.1995). He has also gone out of his way – it should be noted – to eulogise such actively calumniated phenomena as excrement: 'Soft by nature,/non-violent in character,/it is most likely, of all man's works,/ the most peaceable' (*Shit*). Or the anal sphincter, whose functioning is appreciated in terms of Psalm 90: 'And lastly the sphincter,/it often occurs to him, doing its work/without any hitches, by reason of strength/for four times four times five long years' (*Admiration*). It would certainly be hard to accuse this man of one-sidedness.[10]

If Enzensberger is at times unrepentantly scatalogical, he has also engaged point-blank with eschatological themes, scarely common currency in post-war German poetry. In an early satire, God is a kind of Social Darwinist, made in the image of Fifties materialism ('God/who eats like a dog on weekdays, gets eaten on Sunday'; *Whimpering and Firmament*). But quite a few poems written in the past two decades seem intent on mediating in a rather more supralunary sense between the fallen and the celestial. *Grace* begins: 'Another of those foreign words, rarely to be heard/on the telephone. The exhausted vicar/with those syringes and condoms in his front garden/would be embarrassed to mention it.' And *Nimbus* reclaims another word that has fallen into desuetude, finishing up with the speaker contemplating the haloes of saints in a church: '*ungläubig*', the adverb employed here, is tantalisingly equivocal, implying both the inability to believe of an atheist and a believer's admiring incredulity. The references to Mörike's poem *Denk es, o Seele* ('Remember, o soul') can admittedly be construed as straight *memento mori* (as in *Persuasive Talk*) or as entertaining whimsy ('sole' replaces 'soul' in *All the Best*). Yet it is not so easy to shrug off as secular the appearance of an angel, rarely sighted in German poetry since the days of George and Rilke. The angel in question actually invades the work-room of the 'lyric I' – a 'rather commonplace angel,/presumably of lower rank' – and endeavours to pick a quarrel by stressing the degree to which his obstinately silent vis-à-vis is dispensable: 'Of the fifteen thousand hues of blue,/he said, each one makes more of a difference/ /than anything you may do/or refrain from doing,//not to mention the felspar/or the Great Magellanic Cloud [. . .]'(*The Visit*). But the real surprise resides in the ethereal manner in which the encounter is handled: the touch is so heavenly that the piece almost floats away. The discreet sarcasm meted out in the poem addressed directly to God, *Addressee Unknown – Retour à l'expéditeur*, consolingly recalls the Enzensberger we thought we knew; but he has moved on, writing at least half of this epistle which will not arrive with a well-tempered fervour that runs counter to the public doctrine more than one hundred years after Nietzsche's proclamation of God's death:

> [. . .] Many thanks for the four seasons,
> for the number e, for my dose of caffeine,
> and, of course, for the strawberry dish
> painted by Chardin [. . .]

A recent comment demonstrates the pragmatic openness of his position: 'As to religion, it is I think – quite apart from belief or unbelief – an anthropological fact. Not apparently something which can be made to disappear! And it has an evolution all of its own. Why poets should turn a blind eye to that, I cannot see.'[11]

The predominantly religious poems in the last section of *Kiosk* are gathered under the rubric *In der Schwebe* (*In Suspense*, as the official translation has it, but with overtones of 'leaving things open'). Accordingly, one looks in vain for indications of a dogmatic *parti pris*. The penultimate poem, with the mock-authoritative title *Of Life After Death*, sedulously recounts the way non-human life will run riot on earth after man's disappearance, brutally revealing how little our delicate rococo conceits are a match for the dense Transcambodian jungle: 'an extraordinarily sublime spectacle,/but far and wide there is no Piranesi/ to people this Angkor Wat/with shepherds and courtiers on horseback.' On the other hand, the final text – although it is entitled *The Entombment* and starts by looking down at a corpse – has an unmistakable upward momentum: depending on one's viewpoint, the mortal frame in question houses the psyche (psychologists), the soul (priests), the personality (personality managers), the anima, the imago, the Ego, Id and Super-Ego, and so on, and therefore 'The butterfly which is to rise/from this very mixed lot/belongs to a species/about which nothing is known.' Enzensberger would not be Enzensberger if he did not hedge his bets: 'which is to rise' is an impartial-sounding reference to the age-old belief in resurrection rather than a personal profession of faith, and the last words are customarily sceptical. Yet the reader (such is the effect of literature) is left with the indelible mental image of a symbolic butterfly rising – a polyvalent image which leaves open the question of whether lepidopterists have already got the whole of their subject taped.[12] It is as though miracles can happen if one keeps one's eyes or mind open; *Inconspicuous Miracle* reflects on the odds stacked against a seventy-year-old man at a traffic light, who has survived:

> [. . .] heavy barrage near Kursk, a stroke
> in Mallorca, and yet a thousand times
> that deadly roadway crossed
> to buy milk – improbable,
> let's say: ten squared minus nineteen,
> for him to have got through
> as far as today,
> stumbling, but with dry feet
> on his long, long foot journey
> across Lake Gennessaret, of which he knows
> no more than his little dog.

Another anthropological fact which evidently fascinates this author is thought processes – consciousness, and not least its limits. The poem *Homage to Gödel*, first collected in 1971, adapts the distinguished mathematician's theorem to human systems: 'You can investigate your own brain/by means of your own brain:/but not quite./Etc.' And the vertigo brought on by thinking about the thinking which is going on behind the subject's back is a recurrent motif. One recent meditation turns out, aptly enough, to be a circular argument concerning all things that put out twigs and branches, 'not to be grasped,/too variously rich/for this sparrow brain,/this fortuitous link/in an infinite series/which, behind the back/of the one who instead of thinking/is thought, puts out/its twigs and branches' *(Bifurcations)*. Richness and intractability to interpretation: this is Enzensberger's slant on existence in general as on poetry and other particulars. His practical response to such impenetrability is to probe in a provisional spirit, armed only with the precision which also distinguishes his political poems. In *Taxonomy* someone out walking harangues a companion who cannot distinguish between a sedge and a sweet vernal grass or the fescue and the slender brome grass: 'what do you mean by grass?' *On the Algebra of Feelings* breaks through to the specific gravity of emotions – 'embarrassment/ with its pervasive taste of lead'. *The Frogs of Bikini* extrapolates Spinoza's equation '*substantia sive natura sive Deus*' to suit our nuclear times: 'Nn *sive deus*'. And it is strictly in character that Enzensberger should explode the cliché of 'the blank page' in the 1991 poem with that title: 'What you're holding now in your hand is almost white,/but not quite; there is no such thing as a pure white thing [. . .]'. He has proved again and again that scientific precision and lyrical intensity are not strange bedfellows: 'Manuel García,/singing teacher by profession,/was the first (1855)/to see his own vocal chords/vibrate, in a mirror' *(What the Doctors Say)*. And it is this dry-eyed precision which makes it possible for even a variation on the *ubi sunt* topos to remain thoroughly composed: 'What has happened to the bridoons,/the hames and the terrets?/ The cartwright has passed away./Only his name survives,/like an insect congealed in amber,/in the telephone book'(*Vanished Work*). In *Thundery Disturbances on Higher Ground* (1991) Enzensberger comes uncharacteristically close to an explicit *credo*: 'facts', or rather 'givens' ('*Gegebenheiten*'), even if unfathomable, are all that one needs. Apparently repudiating the Heidegger tradition, his narrator professes: 'I bathe in a storm/of uncertainty. Now that's refreshing./One hardly can say that/ about the existence of That Which Exists.'

Enzensberger's 'cerebral' precision does not militate against sensuousness either: poems like *Obsession* and *Fetish* live up to their titles. And *A Sort of Revelation* (1995), which charts the chemical processes underlying someone's reaction to a woman undressing, is briefly in the same league as Herrick and the Keats of *The Eve of St Agnes* before moving on to disarming expressions of gratitude and bafflement:

> [. . .] Fleeting, not to be grasped,
> a sudden gift,
> a sign of returned love
> that none of us deserves.
>
> It passes understanding
> what's so sublime
> about a woman's bare backside.

He can also write love poetry of a kind that would be more intelligible to the troubadours, as in *Pillow Poem* (1991):

Given that you're present right to your
fingertips, that you're seized with desire,
and given the way you bend your knees
and show me your hair,
and given your temperature
and your darkness;
as well as your subordinate clauses,
the insubstantial weight of your elbows,
and also the material soul
that's gleaming in the little hollow
up above your collar-bone;
given that you've gone
and come, and given all
the things that I don't know about you,
my monosyllabic syllables
are not enough, or too much.

Since the Seventies in particular, a different Enzensberger has written so many poems on one specific process – the artistic process as revealed in paintings – that new readers could be forgiven for thinking him a basically pictorial poet. For example, *Gillis van Conninxloo, Landscape. Panel, 65 x 119cm* explores the tension between the reality of life ('Hagar repudiated,/Genesis 20,21,/an abominable divorce story') and the reality of art (thanks to a pinch of powder dissolved in oil, 'I see foaming/white lead, malachite, verdigris,/fresher than water.'). And the imaginary visit to Ingres' atelier again yields admiration for the higher mimesis which art enables: 'the flesh colour smooth/and narcotic, better than Kodak'*(Visiting Ingres)*. Perspective is frequently a preoccupation, as in Enzensberger's other work ('Each one thinks/himself the centre./All but the painter', as the poem on Uccello has it). And so too, as in Enzensberger's writings on literature, is the pleasure principle: *Last Supper. Venetian. Sixteenth Century* delves into the delight the artist experiences even when carrying out commissions relating to endless Crucifixions, Deluges and Massacres of the Innocent.[13] While offering thoughtful recreations of both celebrated and obscure paintings, there is also a sense in which these pictorial poems contribute towards the *ars poetica* Enzensberger has never written.

Why has this poet always been so loth to make overt poetological statements? Maybe because there is something ludicrous about them so far into what Hegel already dubbed the Age of Prose; the self-ironic 'Enzensberger constant' holds that books of poetry, no matter where they are published, have a readership of only +/- 1,354 (*FAZ*, 14.3.1989). At any rate, when he talks about poetry in the abstract it is normally in terms of Tertullian's paradox *credo, quia absurdum*. The *Poem for people who don't read poems* (1960), which gave its name to the 1968 Secker and Warburg bilingual edition translated by Michael Hamburger, Jerome Rothenberg and Enzensberger himself, is about stubbornly scratching words into the sand for someone who – even though his liver too is being consumed by a reach-me-down Promethean eagle – will never get to decipher them. And although a more recent *ad hoc* definition of poetry – 'a way of speaking about things about which one cannot really speak' (*Die Zeit*, 20.1.1995) – may at first sight seem reminiscent of Wittgenstein's epistemological rigorism at the end of the *Tractatus*, it is surely informed by a survivor's determination not to take no for an answer. As he replied to Adorno's anathema to the effect that it is barbaric to write a poem after Auschwitz: 'If we want to continue living, this sentence has got to be disproved'(*Merkur*, 1959, 772).

II

Is there any common ground between these – and other – Enzensbergers? Quite a number of critics have had grave problems living with his 'contradictions' – with the alleged gap between the public and private poet or between the revolutionary and the artist, for example. Peter Demetz's characterisation 'Bucharin and Lord Byron'[14] is charmingly alliterative, but disregards the fact that Enzensberger (unlike Bucharin) did not need to break with Marx because he has always regarded Marxism as a means of social analysis rather than a means to a utopian end, and (unlike Byron) has never been sold on heroes, romantic or otherwise. Questing for contradictions may be a condign occupation in the ivory tower, but it is a simple fact that many major poets have contained multitudes: the 'vituperative' Horace of the *Sermones* and the 'amiable' Horace of the *Epistolae* are just different *personae*, adopted in the interests of different intentions or conventions. If one does require a common denominator for Enzensberger, it is maybe the 20:20 vision which has habitually seen through ideological simplifications; as the narrator in the distantly autobiographical text *The Frogs of Bikini* puts it: 'His favourite drug, he maintains,/is alertness. The daily dose/of ideological cocaine/he'd just as well do without'.

The structural equivalent of such alertness is Enzensberger's predilection for montage. In an 1979 interview he observed that the author's head is invariably full of voices and echoes, that literature is thus a collective enterprise, and that he is not interested in monologue but in the opportunity to work on a part-song basis, especially when dealing with historical processes.[15] An early example is *Remote House* (1964), which contains the strophe: "Caribbean crisis . . . washes whiter/ and whiter and whiter . . . troops ready to fly out . . . / phase three . . . *that's the way I love you* . . . /amalgamated steel stocks are back to par . . ." Pasolini accordingly inferred that Enzensberger had taught professional historians a lesson and initiated a new type of historiography with his documentary novel *The Brief Summer of Anarchy* (1972). The *obiter dictum* in *The Unhappy Ear* (1991) – 'Truth, a montage' – is more than just a boutade.

If one needed an abstract term to epitomise his method, to the extent that it is made manifest in his poems, it would probably be necessary to home in on his agility – his readiness to be surprised by history and to respond flexibly to whatever comes. This brings to mind Friedrich Schlegel's definition of irony: a 'clear awareness of perennial agility [ie, in terms of the intellect], and of infinitely full chaos [ie, plenitude of being]'. If Enzensberger's poems need instructions for use, this definition of irony – rather than the romantic irony of Tieck, the cosmic irony of Hardy and Housman, or the knee-jerk stylistic irony of much recent British poetry[16] – might be a helpful thread to take hold of. Such agility implies a lightness which enables Enzensberger, like Heine before him, to land on his feet whatever the theme. Although his earlier work appeared when confessional poetry was near its apogee, there is a remarkable absence of subjective 'turmoil' (Robert Lowell: *Eye and Tooth*) in this writer. Probably the nearest he ever allows himself to come to self-pity is the bitterly witty Sixties piece called *Compensation*, which numbly reflects on the opportunism of those who keep a close eye on the vacancies column while reading Adorno's *Negative Dialectics* before concluding: 'I'd imagine it was a strain/to be that two-eyed//At times I think, in all modesty,/I must be a cyclops//Then I let the telephone ring out/for days on end.' Not for nothing does Enzensberger repeatedly return to acrobats – to acrobats, moreover, who are decidedly more debonair than the Schopenhauerian figures that people Rilke's fifth Duino elegy. *Bird's Eye View* opens: 'Immune to dizziness/like an old roofer,/agile, not noticed much/by those who have their feet/on the ground of facts', and *Balancing Act* speaks of the 'gyrocompass' deep inside the skull, without which it would not be possible to defy gravity. On reading and rereading these poems, one has to conclude that their author's poise is such that he does not noticeably lose his balance in the course of nearly half a century of walking the poetic tightrope. One could speak of *sprezzatura* here, but if so it would need to be in Castiglione's original sense: elegance as inner equilibrium.

III

Agility is writ large in Enzensberger's formal probings too. A critic has spoken of his 'journalism poetry' (*PNR* 123, 1998, 2), but this is only valid in an etymological, and hence tautological sense: 'Where can we live but days?', as Larkin once put it. True, there is no way that the artistry in his poems calls undue attention to itself. He is not the sort of poet (unlike, say, his near-contemporary Karl Krolow) who is most at home in manifestly virtuoso forms like the sonnet. His one formal (indeed fundamentally Petrarchan) sonnet, from 1991, has been savagely truncated: the acatalectic first and last lines seem to embody the poem's obsessions – silence and transience – and certainly obviate the kind of declamatory quality which Pound believed had already crept into the Italian sonnet by 1300, 'first because of its having all its lines the same length' (*ABC of Reading*, p157). Enzensberger's typical approach is to stretch existing forms, sometimes to the limit and beyond.

One case in point are his *neniae* from 1960, somewhere in the mock-tragic tradition of Catullus (Lesbia's dead sparrow) and Ovid (Corinna's dead parrot), but with a decided difference:

Elegy on Love

This hairy sign
on the toilet wall
who could divine from it
all the songs tears
the storms of desire
the thousand and one nights
in which humankind
like a phosphorescent patch in the ocean
consumed itself
preserved
and forgotten

Nothing here testifies
to those testicled ovaried creatures
born and not born
except for this hairy sign
scratched into
the charred toilet wall

Another instance involves the poems which distantly but distinctly echo classical *terza rima*. Enzensberger possesses all the equipment to be a formalist in the narrower sense, as his technically flawless use of the *terzina* form in a parodistic piece on Brecht – not published in an official collection – makes apparent.[17] But it is simply not his style pedantically to seek to turn the clocks back. It is enough to nonchalantly recast strictly endstopped *terza rima* (*For the Grave of a Peace-loving Man* is one example), and on occasion to add in the *verso di clausola* that rounds off Dante's cantos. Dante, for his part, has clearly been a touchstone for this author at various times. One patiently exasperated 1957 text asks: 'but who can still / wrap up so much hatred in *terza rima*?' And two long poems from his 1960 collection, *Foam* and *Whimpering and Firmament*, read most like two cantos from a latter-day *Inferno* (the hypocrites 'who say Hölderlin and mean Himmler' seem closeish relatives of those who inhabit Dante's eighth circle). It is an atrophied, almost slapstick version of the great Florentine's form which features in the Sixties poem *The Paper Turkey*, but the turbulent descent from the sublime to the banal is obviously part of the message: 'The truly genuine revolutionary/is to be found today on page 30/of the colour supplement [. . .]' Something similar may be true of Enzensberger's epic poem *The Sinking of the Titanic* (1978), which begins in unrhymed *terza rima* and has the historical Dante ghosting right through it. The fact that it consists of 33 cantos (rather than 34, like the *Inferno*) supports the impression gained from a purely semantic reading: we are being offered a kind of reverse journey, from a sublunary *Paradiso* ('the rare light days of euphoria' in Cuba in 1969) to a *Purgatorio* which, although fitted out with all mod cons, offers little prospect of improvement (the snow-bound Berlin of the disenchanted late Seventies). Hell may have been abolished; but so has salvation.

In *Kiosk*, Enzensberger even writes what is, to all intents and purposes, a concrete poem in unrhymed *terza rima*: *Audiosignal of April 14th 1912*, a mightily condensed version of *The Sinking of the Titanic*, if one likes. Each of the five *capitoli* consists of 12 discrete infinitives, while the *verso di clausola* contains just one verb, '*Rauschen*' (the sound of the empty ocean as well as of radio silence), repeated three times. The text is crammed with human activity. At first there are the noises of social intercourse:

Lisping mumbling babbling whispering
snuffling fluting soughing munching
muttering jabbering cooing puffing [. . .]

Later there is a sense of panic. But only on encountering the roar of the engines and the verbs which imply that water is seeping in (in the antepenultimate strophe) does one begin to suspect that it might be the Titanic, or the end of the world itself, which is at issue.[18] Enzensberger insists in *The Watermark of Poetry* that all poems, including legasthenic ones, are distinguished by an 'enigmatic residue', and it would be a bold interpreter who tried to pin down *Audiosignal* to a clear message; what is unquestionable is the intensity – or rather the relentless rise in intensity – in the course of these lines.

Strophic forms are also handled with ingenuity in all periods: one could point to the updating of the sapphic ode in the early poem for a Macedonian shepherd, or to the rhymeless stanzaic structures often employed in later collections. Enzensberger's treatment of one old French form, in *Rondeau* (1971), is particularly instructive: the fastidious refrains of the likes of Deschamps, Marot and Voiture are unsentimentally stripped down to render the vicious circle in which the intellectual was – or felt – trapped during an era of street-fighting men:

> [. . .] But you can't build a house on a mountain.
> So move the mountain.
> It's hard to move mountains.
> So become a prophet.
>
> But you can't hear thoughts.
> So talk.
> It's hard to talk.
> So become what you are
>
> and keep on muttering to yourself,
> useless creature.

In *The Watermark of Poetry* Enzensberger comments on the 'hypnotic' effect which can emanate from repetition of particular words or passages, as well as on the 'type of poetic whispering gallery' which German Baroque poets devised in their echo sonnets. In his own work too, unorthodox variations on the rondeau form are conspicuous by their recurrence, perhaps because they cause – often contradictory – refrains to resonate in the memory. Enzensberger does have certain precursors in this field: Goethe's *Nur wer die Sehnsucht kennt* is essentially a free variation on the rondeau form, and there is also Trakl's *Rondel*.[19] But his tone is unprecedented. The 21 lines of *Historical Process* are held together by three irreconcilable refrains: 'So what', 'That's possible' and 'It doesn't matter about your name'; the poem does come full circle as roundelays traditionally do (the trawlers, ice-bound at the outset, will again be ice-bound when the channel cut by the ice-breaker freezes up), but at a higher level of insight: the subject, whose subjectivity is immaterial, comes to appreciate that he is free, and free to view history as a pageant of incremental progress. The daunting effect in *Manhattan Island*, by contrast, is due to the disparity between the mood of residual hope at the start of each strophe ('When . . . When . . . When . . .') and the – in retrospect, inevitable – outcomes ('bitter ocean . . . bitter bridges . . . bitter sky'). A cursory glance might urge that the following piece is a species of 'journalism poetry', occasioned as it is by reports in some kind of media; but repeated readings again set up echoes which listeners, regardless of their political stance, will not necessarily find easy to suppress:

The Usual Thing

After the Boxer Rising the dowager empress of China
is said to have driven through Peking's streets
in a yellow limousine. On spotting a foreigner
she'd draw back the curtain, make a slight bow
and smile at him. That doesn't matter.

Last week they took away Abdel, my friend.
They kept him locked up for 10 days in a basement. Screamed at him:
You are a CIA agent. Before they let him go
(an error, comrade) they asked him what
his wife was like in bed. That is heavy.

Yarini was the most famous pimp in all Habana.
He was so handsome that they shot him
out in the street. That was 1906.
Halley's comet put in an appearance in 1910.
It's down to return in '86. That doesn't matter.

I found all this out today, the 10th of May '69.
An informative day. And in addition
the day my shoelaces gave up the ghost.
That is heavy, for socialism here in Cuba
cannot replace these laces until '85.

That doesn't matter. That is heavy. That doesn't matter.

In *Ländler* (1980) Enzensberger contrives more cavernous and mournful echoes. With the help of rondeauesque refrains ('Say again', 'When all is said and done', 'the spider in the amber'), the piece reproduces in words the Alpine round-dance which was the precursor of the waltz, this time enacting a view of history as eternal recurrence: '[. . .] Paleontology, the sole science/on which we can count,/consoling and fruitless./It goes round in circles/like that *ländler*/ which, 'when all is said and done',/ doesn't move from the spot.'[20] In the 1995 collection, distant cousins of the rondeau are used to generate different effects again: to capture the anxious reiterations of an 'old whiskered gentleman' sitting knitting in the morning sun (*Nice Sunday*), and to investigate a consciousness apparently striken with Alzheimer's (*Et Ego*).

Enzensberger has also broken ground with more 'open' forms, natural correlatives for the open society for which he has always stood up. The *locus classicus* here is probably *Summer Poem* (1964), a projective text that casts a net across the global village (including the huts where the exploited live), with the effect that 'all distances are the same'. Where Benn, with his regressive proclivities, was a champion of 'absolute' monologues, Enzensberger's texts generally aspire to the condition of dialogue, or polyvocalism ('Vielstimmigkeit'): contradictory voices are admitted to prevent the author from waxing dogmatic or lapsing into isolation.[21] *Lachesis lapponica*, a poem which unfolds at around midnight in a Northern summer, is an illustration of his determination to accommodate incompatible opinions:

> [. . .] I'll cut off your head, bird. (*It's your own.*
> *!Viva Fidel! Better dead than red. Have a break! Ban the bomb!*
> *Über alles in der welt!*) Don't say that. (*You are all that,*
> says the bird, *imagine, you have been that, you are that.*) [. . .]

Other experiments seem bent on unmasking the rhetoric which poses as truth. From his first collection onwards, Enzensberger has frequently set in motion the grammatical *perpetuum mobile*, which ultimately derives from Corbière and which, as in the case of Heissenbüttel, conveys 'moral judgement that could not be conveyed as tellingly in any other way.'[22] One example is *Introduction to Commercial Correspondence*, which begins: 'With very best wishes/With slight sullen coughs/With Christian shivers/With beastly wry faces/With lecherous ruses [. . .]' before spiralling back, thirteen lines later, to the familiar insincere starting-point. More chilling is the technique in *Morphology*, a text which systematically – albeit quite untranslatably – breaks down what in German are matter-of-fact compounds into a combination of noun and deadly adjective: 'In the dead shirts (shrouds)/Rest the blind dogs (guide-dogs)/Round the sick cash desks (health insurance schemes)/ Walk the sore washers (those who wash wounds) [. . .]' There is an affinity with concrete poetry, but the political charge tends to be higher: *Proposal for Penal Reform* is a discomfiting potpourri of items from the German Criminal Code, and *Berlin Model* – also published for the first time in 1967 – goes as far as to reproduce a newspaper article on a new class of industrial electronics with integrated circuits, exploiting the ambiguity latent in language to suggest what such 'totalitarian' systems lead to on a human level ('Fortunately there is no need with this technology to make allowances either for tolerances or parasitic elements'). Enzensberger's search for new avenues of expression even throws up a neo-Aztec text, *The Festival of Flowers*. And one of the last poems in *Music of the Future* is a eulogy of Aeolian forms – such as shifting seif dunes, 'Pure art, which is in no need of an artist'. Such *poésie pure*, written and then at once erased by the wind, is doubtless at some considerable remove from what Parisian neo-Platonists like Valéry had in mind. Be that as it may, while German theorists have been deliberating on the merits of the long 'emancipatory' poem (W Höllerer) vis-à-vis the short 'hermetic' lyric (K Krolow), Enzensberger has quietly been getting on with the task of putting both these and other forms (such as the ballad: *Mausoleum. Thirty Seven Ballads from the History of Progress*, Frankfurt am Main, 1975) to the test.

IV

In the examples given to date, the English texts have been taken for granted. In fact, they spring from an ongoing collaboration between two master craftsmen which goes back to the start of the Sixties: Bloodaxe has brought out a total of 141 texts, mostly by Michael Hamburger but as many as 30% by Enzensberger himself. The quality of these translations is such that one could spend pages listing special felicities, such as Hamburger's choice of adverb in the first strophe of *The Midwives* ('In buzzing clusters out they swarm / in the grey light of daybreak clamber / limberly over hedges and bridges . . .') and the way he makes a specifically British poem out of *Short History of the Bourgeoisie* by substituting 'Tudor fireplaces' for '*Renaissancekamine*', or Enzensberger's cummingsesque play 'Man manhandled' in his version *Limbic System*.[23] Particularly suggestive are the cases where the two poets' preoccupations coincide exactly: *Norwegian Timber* would strike most Anglo-Saxon readers as a Hamburger poem in its own right.

If one has to express any disappointment, it is that the collaborators decided – presumably in the interests of consistency – not to print parallel versions in those cases where both had produced translations. For these would have permitted greater insight into their particular translation technique, and – without question – into poetic translation technique in general. Let us look, for example, at Hamburger's version of *Abtrift*, a poem which supplies the title for the last section of *Music of the Future*, alongside Enzensberger's previously unpublished counterpart:

Leeway	**Drift**
The brain on its descent,	The brain in descent,
lower and lower.	sinking by the minute.
Against the tension wires	The downdraught tearing away
the down-draught tugs.	at the bracing-wires,
The rudder flutters,	the rudder fluttering,
veers	swerving,
'by itself'.	all on its own.
A music too:	Another kind of music:
rushing air,	the rush of air,
creaking timbers.	the wood creaking.
There's a crack in the spar,	A crackle in the cross-beams,

in the ear, in the head.	in the ear, in the skull.
Painless suction,	Painless suction,
self-oblivious,	oblivion,
solemnly weightless	solemn, easy glide
gliding towards	into the dark.
the darker place.	
[MH]	[HME]

The severely reined-in rhythm of the German original makes it distantly resemble the *Parzenlied* in Goethe's *Iphigenie*. But where the latter harps on the sombre fate of mankind, Enzensberger's text – a product of the same century as Saint-Exupéry's *Vol de Nuit* – has a more reckless, existential tonality. Both translations accurately render the overall gesture, but Hamburger's is undoubtedly the more faithful. This translator characteristically holds the highly individual creative writer in himself in check in order to do justice to the quiddity of the foreign text: the ironising inverted commas in line 7 are preserved, as are the 'falling' dactylic rhythms *in extremis* in the final lines, and the fact that the version has the same number of lines as the original is a small but significant detail. Enzensberger for his part is freer, bringing out the drama of tension and release by opting for frenetic present participles in the opening lines and stupefying trochees for the final passage into night.[24] The unobtrusive skill of these experienced *fabbri* comes out most obviously in their response to the narcotic assonance pervading the final sentence of the German text ('SchmerzlOser SOg, / selbstvergessen, / fEIerlich lEIchtes / GlEIten, dem / DUnkleren zU.'). Hamburger fashions an equivalent by means of hypnotic repetition (painLESS, oblivIOUS, weightLESS) and by the solemnly weightless gliding inherent in his curtailed dactylic hexameters; Enzensberger does so by virtue of vocalic rhyme (suction/oblivion) and through the alluring pattern of vowels in the last two lines, swallowing up the world in a Baudelairean yawn.

Let us also take a look at Hamburger's version of *Das Gift*, another poem from the final section of *Music of the Future*, and at Enzensberger's unpublished parallel version:

The Poison	**The Poison**
Not as it used to be, round,	Not the way it used to be, round,
little, a grain, sealed	tiny, a grain, sealed
like a berry, a pea,	like a berry, like a pea,
tiny, concealed in a ring,	smallish, hidden away in a ring,
a capsule, private, minimal,	a capsule, private, minimal,
secret like an *idée fixe*,	secret like an *idée fixe*,

but manifest like the sea,	no, open now, evident
ponderous and normal,	like an ocean, weighty, normal
widely distributed, like the wind	and profligate, like the wind
unleashed, cloudy, odourless	unfettered, odourless, cloudy,
and as impalpable, omni-	unseizable, omnipresent –
present as God was once	the way God used to be,
who, a private grain,	he who now weighs less and less,
little, weighs less and less,	a private grain, like a pea,
like a pea, secret,	secretly, like a berry
like a deadly nightshade seed	of belladonna buried away
in one's breast, sealed	in the heart,
like an *idée fixe*.	like an *idée fixe*.
[MH]	[HME]

Of course it is not possible either to render the quasi-anagram GifT/ GotT, which gives the German original its poignant point, or to convey the implications of the fact that the original phrase behind 'as impalpable' and 'unseizable' in line 11 ('*ebensowenig zu fassen*') is a sardonic echo of Hölderlin's hymn *Patmos* ('Near / But hard to grasp is God'). Nevertheless, the strong overall pattern (three six-line stanzas with three similes apiece), the urgent underlying rhythm, and the hermetic compression (the Sublime operates 'with heavy blows', as J G Sulzer put it at the end of the 18th century, and we are certainly dealing here with a laconic, modern version of the *genus sublime*) come across undiminished in both these versions. So too does the unrelenting, if unrhetorical *amplificatio*: poison was only concealed *on* the chest whereas God, that ultimate potion, has now to be hidden deep down *within* a person's breast. Again Hamburger shows greater loyalty to the original, adhering strictly to the line-disposition and implementing the – by historical standards – blasphemous enjambment '*all-gegenwärtig*' (how far away one is from Klopstock's 1749 alcaic ode *An Gott*, in which the author confesses how deeply moved he is by the awareness of his Author's omnipresence!). One way Hamburger adds value is by binding together the capsule-like text with the aid of rhyme and pararhyme (st.1: be, berry, pea, tiny; st.2: sea, cloudy, omni-; st.3: pea, deadly). Enzensberger, it turns out, does the same, indeed to an even more insistent extent: way, be, tiny, berry, pea, away, weighty, cloudy, way, be, he, pea, secretly, berry, away. But, again, his version is more of a variation or imitation than his friend's: one need only point to the more conversational structure that has been imported ('no . . .', and the dash which precedes the audacious leap in line 12); the decision to render '*offenbar*' by means of two adjectives ('open . . . evident'); the Miltonic 'profligate' in contrast to Hamburger's neutral rendering of 'breit verteilt'; the change in word-order (on rhythmical grounds, it would seem) which leads to 'odourless, cloudy'; and the liberties taken with word-order in the last strophe. One enrichment is 'smallish': the refusal to be uncool even when dealing with matters of such import. Another is the shift from 'hidden away' to 'buried away', underlining the crescendo which the poem is plotting. Another is the compelling alliteration 'like a berry / of belladonna buried away...' Suffice it to say that students of translation would have reason to be grateful to Enzensberger, to Hamburger and to Bloodaxe if future editions of these collections were expanded to include all extant versions.[25]

V

Are there any lapses in these two new volumes? Well, there appears to be a printing error in *Kiosk*: 'May', in the German original, has changed to 'April' in the title *Audiosignal of April 14th 1912*; but if it is correct (as was argued above) that the Titanic is the covert subject of the poem in question, the typo was in fact in Suhrkamp's original German. The reviewer has also got one regret: that Enzensberger's debut collection, *The Wolves Defended*, is not represented; with its 'friendly', 'sad' and 'angry' poems, it contains the whole poet in embryonic form. Otherwise one can only feel gratitude – and admiration – that the whole of *Kiosk* and such significant portions of the other collections have been coaxed – or, to use one of Enzensberger's own terms for poetic translation, smuggled – into English.[26]

What general conclusions can be drawn? That Enzensberger has a singular range, 'from intestinal flora to the galaxies', to quote a formulation from *Music of the Future*. In the Nineties, he has – to give just three examples – stimulated German domestic policy with his essays on civil war, adapted Spanish Baroque drama, and scripted a parody of the ubiquitous modern talkshow, in which various guests from the 1820s lay into Goethe, a kind of Godot who never quite makes it into the TV studio. It is hard to think who else since Heine has straddled so many divides. And one may feel that there is some type of poetic justice in the coincidence that his surname spans both the scholastic Latin for 'being', the species of Buddhism that seeks to discover the transcendent in the transient, and the German word for mountains, that so Rousseauistic phenomenon that he has looked at so scientifically: 'What does slowness mean/ for a mountain?' (*Flight of Ideas III*). Perhaps his poetry can be regarded as a kind of cocktail: 1 shot of Archilochos, 1 of Pindar, 1 of Callimachos, 1 of Bion, 1 of Lucretius, 1 of Catullus, 1 of Horace, 1 of Petrarch, 1 of Villon, 1 of Góngora, 1 of Rochester, 1 of von Besser, and so on. If so, there are a number of ingredients which cannot be traced to any predecessor. There is also a certain irrepressible freshness, the sort of thing which – not just for Pound (*ABC of Reading*, pp13ff) – makes a classic classic.

Notes

1   cf the correspondence with Hannah Arendt, *Merkur*, 1965, 380-85, and the remark 'Il peggio negli anni '50 era proprio il silenzio', *agorá europa*, 9/1989, 35.

2   *Hans Magnus Enzensberger*, ed R Grimm, Frankfurt am M, 1984, p115.

3   Like Pound before him ('Thomas Hardy's Noble Dames and Little Ironies will find readers despite all the French theories in the world'; *ABC of Reading*, London, 1979, p193), Enzensberger has little truck with 'all this talk about the disappearance of the subject, the I. It is a French fashion that has colonised the academic world' (interview with Peter Forbes, *The Independent on Sunday*, quoted from *Bloodaxe Catalogue*, 1996). The New York poem *Leaving Aside*, written in the Seventies and intriguingly revised in *Kiosk*, is perhaps the clearest statement of his commitment to mortal details: '[. . .] anyone who can't leave those aside/is no theorist.'

4   There is a prose parallel in a 1965 letter to H Arendt: the *argumentum ad oculos* 'I see . . . I see', attacking abstract meliorism by appeal to the concrete misery of Africa, Southern Asia and Latin America (cf *Hans Magnus Enzensberger*, opcit, p84). This does not stop Enzensberger, in a different context, from writing like a dark – if *désinvolte* – seer: 'Punch tape's fluttering down/It's snowing electron braille/From every cloud nine/fall digital prophets' *(Braille*, 1964).

5   HM Enzensberger, *Gedichte. Die Entstehung eines Gedichts*, 2nd ed, Frankfurt am M 1962, p42.

6   R Wellek and A Warren, *Theory of Literature*, Harmondsworth, 1973, p189.

7   *Mein Gedicht ist mein Messer*, ed H Bender, Munich, 1961, pp144ff.

8   Rainer Nägele,'Das Werden im Vergehen oder Das untergehende Vaterland: Zu Enzensbergers Poetik und poetischer Verfahrensweise', *Hans Magnus Enzensberger*, opcit, p223.

9   *Poems of Paul Celan*, tr M Hamburger, London, 1988, p227.

10   Perhaps his most vitriolic performance, *Language of the Country*, carries an epigraph from Pliny's *Natural History* concerning an Athenian author who was out to present his fellow countrymen as they seemed to him – at the same time fickle, choleric, unjust, merciful, compassionate, lofty, humble, and so on. And doing justice to both sides of issues has evidently been Enzensberger's own ambition ever since *The Wolves Defended Against the Lambs* (1957), in which a large proportion of the blame for the Third Reich is laid at the door of those whose indolent obedience let the Nazis in.

11   'Was die Religion angeht: sie ist, denke ich, ganz abgesehen von Glaube oder Unglaube, eine anthropologische Tatsache. Offenbar nicht zum Verschwinden zu bringen! Und sie hat ihre eigene Evolution. Warum die Dichter das ignorieren sollten, kann ich nicht einsehen' (letter to the author, 26.12.1998).

12   Wittgenstein remarks in the *Philosophical Investigations* on the role images can play when it comes to conveying such ideas as the survival of the soul after death (*Werkausgabe*, vol 1, Frankfurt am M, 1990, p495).

13   One example of Enzensberger's commitment to the pleasure principle in literature is his essay *On the difficulty and pleasure of translating Molière (Die Zeit,*

7.12.1979); another is the alternative title to *The Watermark of Poetry* (see note 17 below), which runs *The Art and the Pleasure of Reading Poems*.

14 P Demetz, *Die süße Anarchie. Deutsche Literatur seit 1945*, Frankfurt am M/ Berlin, 1970, p112.

15 *Hans Magnus Enzensberger*, opcit, pp131ff.

16 cf Michael Schmidt, *Lives of the Poets*, London, 1998, p851.

17 This first saw the light of day in his mystification *The Watermark of Poetry* (1985), an exuberantly erudite ABC of poetic technique ranging from the cento to versus cancellati – and including such wonders as Ungaretti in semaphore and the German Baroque poet Harsdörffer in ASCII code – to which he contributes under pseudonyms like Andreas Thalmayr and the self-deprecatory anagram Serenus M Brezengang. This annotated anthology reveals the depth of Enzensberger's interest in both possible and impossible poetic forms; that he lives down on the street as much as up in the study can be gauged from his 'translation' of a Petrarchan sonnet by Rückert into pidgin – more specifically, guestworker – German: 'Amara, du nix gut, du nix gut machen . . .' (roughly: 'Amara, you no good, no good do woman . . .'). A rewarding study could be written on the submerged formalism in Enzensberger's official poetry. His use of rhyme, in the Fifties and later, would be one factor that would repay careful attention. It is not easy to think who else could have rhymed 'Marx' with the genitive of the German word for coffin ('Sargs'), as he does in one of the songs written for Ingrid Caven. And the Black-English couplets in the twentieth canto of *The Sinking of the Titanic* pulsate with anarchic energy: '[. . .]That's when the Captain's daughter came up on the deck/with her hands on her pussy and drawers round her neck./She said, 'Shine, Shine, save poor me,/give you more pussy than any black man see.[. . .]' (HM Enzensberger, *The Sinking of the Titanic. A Poem*, translated by the author, Manchester, 1981, pp54ff; the Bloodaxe *Selected Poems* contains selected episodes from this epic poem, but the reader is referred to the Carcanet edition for the full text.)

18 Brian McCredie sees a distant (semantic and formal) parallel in Marcus Aurelius' *Meditations*: 'Men and women busy marrying, bringing up children, sickening, dying, fighting, feasting, chaffering, farming, flattering, bragging, envying, scheming, calling down curses, grumbling at fate, loving, hoarding, coveting thrones and dignities. Of all that life, not a trace survives today' (tr Staniforth).

19 An English version, by Ruth and Matthew Mead, was published in *Agenda* 32/ 2 (1994), 22.

20 Enzensberger reconstitutes musical forms on other occasions too, for instance in *Scherzo* (1957) and *Valse triste et sentimentale* (first published 1972). The plangent *Finnish Tango* (first published 1976) lingers particularly long in the memory – '[. . .] how bright/the summer is here and how short' – and it is a pity that Hamburger's equally resonant version has not found its way into the Bloodaxe *Selected*.

21 *Hans Magnus Enzensberger*, opcit, p132.

22 Michael Hamburger, *The Truth of Poetry*, Harmondsworth, 1972, pp336ff. Hamburger finds a fitting equivalent for the at once tragic and farcical inexorability inherent in Heissenbüttel's experiments with the grammatical

perpetuum mobile (*Class Analysis, The New Age, The Future of Socialism* etc) in H Heissenbüttel, *TEXTS,*

tr M Hamburger, London, 1977.

23 There is also something to be learnt from the way Enzensberger translates his deconstruction of what has become a German proverb: Rilke's line 'Wer spricht von Siegen? Überstehn ist alles' ('Who speaks of victory? Endurance is all.'), which accompanied soldiers into battle in both world wars, metamorphoses into the German equivalent of 'And that endurance isn't all but nothing at all/oh we know' in the original of *Song for those who Know,* but vanishes without a trace in the English version. Some things are simply too culture-specific.

24 The evidence is that Enzensberger translates more freely because he does not feel beholden to his own brain-child. In his numerous versions from other poets, his way is to carefully match each effect, one example being his rendering of the lines 'Regard that woman/Who hesitates toward you in the light of the door' from Eliot's *Rhapsody on a Windy Night:* 'Sieh diese Frau/wie sie dir zuzaudert [!] unter der hellen Tür.'

(TS Eliot, *Gesammelte Gedichte 1909-1962,* ed E Hesse, Frankfurt am M, 1988, p29). Hamburger's position on translation (faithfulness to the spirit of the original, which can entail instinctive liberties) comes out clearly in his conversation with Edwin Honig (M Hamburger,*Testimonies. Selected Shorter Prose 1950-1987,* Manchester, 1989, pp243-256).

25 Both unpublished versions are quoted here with the permission of Hans Magnus Enzensberger.

26 Enzensberger's versions from Edward Lear appeared under the title *Edward Lears kompletter Nonsens. Ins Deutsche geschmuggelt von Hans Magnus Enzensberger* (Frankfurt am M, 1977).

Review

by Ruth Fainlight

The Defiant Muse: Hebrew Feminist Poems from Antiquity to the Present
A bilingual anthology edited by Shirley Kaufman,
Galit Hasan-Rokem, Tamar S Hess
The Feminist Press of City University. New York, 1999
ISBN 1 55861 224 6

Until very recently, Hebrew was reserved for religious purposes only. Talmudic study and the language of liturgy were not for women; special prayers for women were usually written in Yiddish, the 'mother tongue'. That certain women dared to study and master Hebrew well enough to write verse in it made these writers early feminists – women who could express ideas and feelings in the language of men. And paradoxically, as the poet Yehuda Leib Gordon said, 'The woman writes with the pen of a bird, the man with a pen of iron and lead'.

Claims have been made that some Biblical texts, such as the first-person passages of the Books of Ruth and Esther, were written by women. The Song of Deborah, said to be the oldest long poem in the Hebrew Bible, seems to open with a double attribution: 'Deborah and Barak, son of Abinoam.' Here the feminine form of the verb 'to sing' implies Deborah's primacy, because Biblical Hebrew verb forms often conform, in case and gender, to the 'more important' of two actors. The main post-Biblical Hebrew text is the Talmud, in both its Babylonian and Palestinian versions reflecting the scholarly debates from which it emerged. It was compiled by men, but an involvement by women can be inferred from introductory formulae, such as 'mother told me' or 'the women of Shkanziv say', which precede sections dealing with healing, nurturing, sex, and magic traditions.

Centuries later, Dunash ben Labrat was the first great Jewish poet of the 'golden age' of Moslem southern Spain, but a poem by his wife (whose own name is lost) is the first Hebrew poem by a woman to give lyric expression to her intimate cares (tr. Peter Cole):

Will her love remember his graceful doe,
    her only son in her arms as he parted?
On her left hand he placed a ring from his right,
    on his wrist she placed her bracelet.

As a keepsake she took his mantle from him,
    and he in turn took hers from her.
He won't settle in the land of Spain,
    though its prince give him half his kingdom.

A tradition of monasticism made it possible for Christian women to develop their creativity as nuns, but there was no institutionalised way for Jewish women to escape matrimonial obligations, and after the expulsion of the Jews from Spain in 1492, writing in Hebrew by Jewish women almost disappeared. In the sixteenth century, Asenath, daughter of a rabbi and widow of another rabbi in Kurdistan, left a long poem of lament and petition in the form of a rhymed letter. There are a few seventeenth- and eighteenth-poems in Yiddish by women from Central and Eastern Europe, and the female tradition of oral poetry in various North African Judeo-Arabic dialects is well-known, but the only two poems in Hebrew that have been discovered from that period were written in Morocco by Freyha Bat Avraham Bar-Adiba.

Rachel Morpurgo (1790-1871), the first modern woman poet to write in Hebrew, belonged to the Italian Jewish community. Though her poetry was conventional in form, its message was radically feminist, a protest against the status of women in Jewish religious culture as 'non-persons' ('On Hearing She Had Been Praised in the Journals'; tr. Peter Cole):

My soul sighs, fate brings only trouble,
my spirit was lifted and I grew bold.
I heard a voice: 'Your poem is gold.
Who like you has learned to sing, Rachel?'

[. . . . . .]

I've looked to the north, south, east, and west:
a woman's word in each is lighter than dust.
Years hence, will anyone really remember

her name, in city or province, any more
than a dead dog. Ask: the people are sure:
a woman's wisdom is only in spinning wool.

Signed: *Wife of Jacob Morpurgo, stillborn.*

Because Hebrew was not a secular language, a secular aesthetic which could be related to the Hebrew canon had to be developed. The fact that women had been prevented from reading and writing in

Hebrew became an advantage. It was thought that they would be able to liberate Hebrew idiom from tradition because they were unaware of its constraints. But for decades most women were more inclined to write prose, since poetry exposed its author in a way that was in opposition to the code of modesty women were conditioned to obey.

The first poet in this anthology who spoke Hebrew as a child is Esther Raab (1894-1981). Until the 1950s, she, Rahel (1890-1931) and Leah Goldberg (1911-1970) were regarded as the emblematic women poets of Ottoman and Mandatory Palestine and Israel's first years. Stanzas from Rahel's 'A Way of Speaking' are a good example of the freshness (and also the ironic intelligence, often ignored) of her writing (tr. Shirley Kaufman):

> I know many fancy ways to speak
> endless and elegant.
> They go mincing down the street,
> their glance is arrogant.
>
> But I like a way of speaking
> as innocent as a baby, as modest
> as dust. I can say countless words.
> So I don't say them.

Probably the recent women poets best known outside Israel are Dahlia Ravikovitch (1936-) and Yona Wallach (1941-1985). Ravikovitch skilfully combines classical mythology and Biblical references to comment on her own life and the political situation with a mixture of bitterness and tenderness, as in 'A Mother Walks Around' (tr. Chana Bloch and Ariel Bloch), about a woman who carries a dead foetus that will be stillborn in due time – "She won't have to worry about his future":

> And this is the history of the child
> who was killed in his mother's belly
> in the month of January, 1988,
> for reasons of state security.

Wallach died at the age of 41 but the influence of her vivid, radical and iconoclastic poetry is still apparent in much poetry by women writing today. Almost half of this comprehensive anthology is by poets of the same generation as, or younger than Ravikovitch and Wallach, from Shulamith Hareven, born in 1932, to Rahel Chalfi, born in 1941, and the youngest of all, Sharon Hass, born in 1966.

As always with a good anthology, one wants more examples from the work of each contributor, and an even wider selection. Apart from this quibble, I have only praise for this handsome book. The editors' Introduction to three thousand years of material is fascinating and informative about the poets, their critical reception, and the changing position of women poets in Israel. The range of translators is impressive, and to a non-reader of Hebrew their English versions read like real poems. Yona Wallach's characterisation of the Hebrew language, quoted at the head of the Note on Translation, is so apposite that I quote it again here (tr. Lisa Katz):

Hebrew is a woman bathing
Hebrew is Batsheva clean
Hebrew is an unsculpted sculpture
with tiny beauty marks and stretch marks from giving birth
the older she gets the more beautiful she is
her judgement is sometimes prehistoric

The full text of 'A Mother Walks Around' appears in Palestinian and Israeli Poets (MPT 14), *along with other poems by some of the Israeli women poets mentioned here.*

MPT original series (1966-1983)

Some copies of most issues in the original series of *MPT* are still available. They include, amongst others:

No 4 – Greek
Nos 5 and 35 – Czech
No 6 – Russian
No 8 – Slovene
No 10 – Turkish
No 11 – Scandinavian
No 13/14 – Portuguese
No 15 – Arabic
No 18 – Mexican; Soviet Georgian
No 19/20 – International Writing Program, University of Iowa
No 22 – Israeli
No 26 – Italian
No 27/28 – Dutch
No 30 – Icelandic
No 37/38 – Francophone poets of Africa
No 40 – Celan, 19th-century Russian
No 41/42 – Translation theory and practice
MPT Yearbook, 1983

Full details and prices from Norma Rinsler, School of Humanities, King's College London, Strand, London WC2R 2LS.